BBC

GARDENERS' WORLD

Through the Years

GAY SEARCH

CARLTON
BOOKS

THIS IS A CARLTON BOOK

This edition first published by Carlton Books Limited 2006
An imprint of the Carlton Publishing Group,
20 Mortimer Street,
London
W1T 3JW

First published by Carlton Books Limited in 2003

A CIP catalogue record for this book is available from the British
Library.

ISBN 1 84442 416 2

Editor: Lorna Russell
Managing Art Director: Jeremy Southgate
Design: Dan Witchell
Production: Lisa Moore

Printed in the UK

Carlton Books would like to thank the following sources for their kind
permission to reproduce the photographs in this book.

Amateur Gardening p9, 52, 56b; BBC p8,56b, 88br, 152/JB; Mark
Bolton p146,147;Jonathan Buckley p3, 24, 27, 34, 80, 81, 104,
105, 114, 115, 117, 164 t, 184, 185; *BBC Gardeners' World*
magazine p4 Sara Heneghan, 10, 17 Jonathan Buckley, 19 Giles
Park, 23, 47, 48-49JB, 62, 63, 64 Justyn Willmsore, 66JB, 67JB,
68JW, 69, 82, 85, 86-87JB, 90, 91bSH, 92SH, 93tl, bl, 95t, 96JW,
97JW.100, 102JW, 103tr, bmWilliam Shaw, 106, 107, 110, 111,
136, 137, 150WS, 151t, brWS, 154-155WS, 157WS, 160, 168, 169,
172, 174, 176, 177, 179, 191 Tim Sandall;Catalyst Television p 25,
26b, 29l, 30, 33t, 34, 37l, 38, 41t, 42, 77l, 88bl, 89, 95m, b, 99,
103tl, bl, br, 109, 130, 131, 133, 135, 149, 151bl, 153, 158, 159,
164ml, mr, 165ml, br, 166, 175, 180, 181, 190; Robert Challinor
p11, 46, 54; John Glover p83; Stephen Hamilton p14, 15, 16, 58,
59, 61, 70, 88t, 91t, 93br, 162/163, 170/171; Jerry Harpur p22-23,
40, 72-73, 118, 120, 121, 123, 128, 187; Marcus Harpur p28, 31,
33;122 Holt Studios International 188/189; Jacquie Hurst p37, 39;
Anne Hyde p78, 79; IPC Magazines Ltd p50; Carl and Pat Jameson
p51t; Andrew Lawson p 74, 75, 124, 125, 142, 143, 144, 165tr, tl,
mr, bl, 182, 183, 178b.; Anthony Lord p138-139, 140, 141; Vilma
Laryea p1, 18, 98, 151bl mr; Clive Nichols 26,32, 36, 41 43,
112/113, 145, 186; *Radio Times*/Mark Harrison p101, 108, 127;
Rex Features p20; Ron Scamp p20r; Royal Horticultural Society
p178t; Peter Seabrook p56t, m, 57; Jason Smalley p148; Chris
Spencer p76, 77rt; Connie Thrower p51b; Jo Whitmore p167
The Publisher is unable to identify the copyright holder of the
photograph on p131, to whom acknowledgement is made

Garden Designers
p3 Alan Gray and Graham Robeson; p128/129 Terry Welch; p72/73
Dan Pearson

Acknowledgements
Grateful thanks for the memories are due to: Barrie Edgar, John
Kenyon, Dennis Gartside, Jean Laughton, Peter Seabrook, Riet Billitt,
Glen Jones, Margaret Thrower (to whom thanks are also due for
permission to quote from Percy Thrower's books) as well presenters,
past and present.

Thanks must also go to Adam Pasco, editor of Gardeners' World
magazine for his encouragement and advice, and to Anne Millman
and her team for invaluable help in providing some of the pictures.

All the garden photographers whose work makes the book a
visual feast.

Dan Witchell of Kemistry for the stylish design and to Steve
Hooley, also of Kemistry, for his electronic wizardry.

Jonathan Goodman of Carlton Books for his faith in the project,
and to Lorna Russell and Clare Baggaley for seeing it through.

And finally to Robin Wood of BBC Books for allowing the book
to happen.

Contents

How It Started

Gardeners' World is one of the longest-running factual television series ever made, and certainly the oldest gardening programme. Over the years, it has reflected the many changes that have taken place in gardens and gardening and, just as important, our attitudes to them. While initially gardening was an end itself, now for many people for whom the garden is valuable outside living space, it is simply a means to an end. But no matter at what level we garden, whether we're experts or novices, totally dedicated or doing the bare minimum, it taps into something very deep in all of us, which is why viewers have a relationship with the programme that is unlike any other.

Gardeners' World Through the Years looks back at the people, both presenters and guests, and perhaps most importantly, some the plants and gardens that have given the programme its special place in viewers' affections.

Gay Search

**A Royal Gardener: the young
Percy Thrower at Windsor.**

When colour television began in the late 1960s, the BBC realised quickly that the ideal subject matter for colour transmissions – apart from snooker, that is – was gardening. The BBC had made gardening programmes since before the war, but techniques were demonstrated with chalk on a blackboard before the advent of outside broadcasts, and the setting up of the first television garden at Alexandra Palace with Fred Streeter as the presenter.

During the 1950s and 1960s, Percy Thrower had become a very popular presenter, first on radio and then on television in *Gardening Club*, based in a BBC studio with its famous glassless greenhouse and a ton of soil carted in and out along with plants that were replanted every week.

With the new era in broadcasting about to begin, in 1968 it was decided to launch a new half-hour programme in colour, *Gardeners' World*. The first-ever programme came from the Oxford Botanical Gardens. According to the first

producer, Paul Morby, the point was to show off the joys of colour by filming the amazing blue tropical water lilies in the glasshouse. These water lilies are night-flowering though, and close around ten o'clock in the morning. By the time they had got all the gear out of the huge vans and assembled, the water lilies had closed, so they filmed an item on loofahs instead.

While the decidedly stagey studio 'garden' was acceptable in black and white, Paul Morby, the producer, felt that, for colour, the programme needed a real garden as its base. So a rundown allotment next to the Birmingham Botanical Gardens was acquired, soon expanding to six allotments. But with no one to look after it between recording days, nature took its course and it became overgrown with weeds. With the letters of complaint flooding in, Percy decided that he had had enough and, after a brief hiatus, the programme's location moved to The Magnolias, Percy's own garden in Shrewsbury, which he had created from a field between 1963 and 1968.

BELOW: Fred Streeter in the first TV garden at Alexandra Palace.

ABOVE: The crew at The Magnolias. Bill Duncalf is in the centre in the striped shirt.

In 1969, Percy Thrower was joined by his old friend and broadcasting colleague, Arthur Billitt, whose garden, Clack's Farm near Droitwich, became the programme's second base. Bill Duncalf, by now the programme's producer, had been to see Arthur the previous autumn, to ask whether he could create a fruit and vegetable garden on some uncultivated land, ready for the cameras the following March. Since that was only six months away, and mostly winter, this was a real challenge. Despite a major scare in February, when Arthur learnt that the billing in the *Radio Times*, already gone to press, would tell viewers that apples, pears and plums would feature and he hadn't yet planted any, the garden was still ready on time.

Gardeners' World also visited large gardens around the country. They had to be big to accommodate the outside broadcast unit, which travelled in three or four huge vans the size of pantechnicons with a crew of around thirty people. In addition to cameramen, sound recordists and engineers, there were teams of riggers who manipulated the cables – in those days the enormous, heavy cameras, which took four men to lift, were physically attached to the outside broadcast scanner by heavy cables as thick as your wrist. By comparison, the production team was

minute. There was just a producer, initially Paul Morby, then the late Bill Duncalf, followed in 1972 by Barrie Edgar, sometimes a director and a production assistant. Any research was done by the presenters themselves, although, of course, they were hugely knowledgeable in the first place.

The gardens also had to have paths wide and strong enough for the cameras to trundle along. As they discovered on the first shoot at Clack's Farm, rain, grass paths and heavy cameras on dollies are not a good combination, so the grass was soon replaced by concrete slabs.

'There were lots of marvellous gardens I would have loved us to visit,' said Barrie Edgar, now in his 80s ,'but it was just impossible with the big heavy cabled equipment we used then. On my very last programme from Clack's Farm in 1979, as a special treat, I was allowed to play with one of the handheld cameras that were just coming into the newsroom then. I thought, "What gardens we could have covered if we'd had some of these!"'

Since the cost of the outside broadcast operation was high, the gardens chosen also had to be large enough to sustain two complete half-hour programmes.

For the same budgetary reasons, when *Gardeners' World* came from The Magnolias or Clack's Farm, two programmes were recorded on the same day, usually a Tuesday, one in the morning, one in the afternoon. In order to be as topical as possible, the first programme would go out on the Friday, three days later. Then they just had to hope that there were no dramatic changes in the weather so that a programme recorded in glorious early spring sunshine didn't go out ten days later when the country was covered in late snow.

'They were planned about four weeks in advance,' recalled Barrie Edgar, 'primarily so that the *Radio Times* could print at least some details of the content. After we'd finished the two programmes at The Magnolias I'd sit down with Percy and we'd talk about what we'd be doing in a month's time. I was a keen gardener so I had an idea of what we ought to be covering, and I relied heavily on Percy's books. We never had a disagreement, though sometimes Percy might say, "Oh not pelargonium cuttings again!" But that's gardening – it is cyclical and I used to say to him, "I'm a keen gardener but I like to reminded of what I should be doing, and when. And don't forget there are new gardeners coming to the programme every year."'

Percy used to appear with Arthur at Clack's Farm, where they featured fruit and veg, and occasionally Arthur would visit The Magnolias, where the ornamental garden was the focus. Disagreements between Arthur the philosopher and Percy the pragmatist about gardening and life soon became an important part of the programme's texture.

LEFT: Percy and Arthur getting
their hands dirty at Clack's farm.

ABOVE: Concrete slabs bore the heavy weight of camera and dolly.

There were also occasional visiting experts. One was Welshman, Clay Jones, for example, who had been broadcasting on the Welsh-language radio programme *Garddio* for years, and who had made many appearances on *Gardening Club*. Another was Geoffrey Smith, superintendent of Harlow Carr, who became a frequent guest, mainly at Clacks Farm, and especially when alpine plants were involved.

In the spring of 1976, Percy Thrower signed a contract to appear in TV commercials, promoting ICI's Garden Plus and Rose Plus fertiliser. He had been working with Plant Protection, a subsidiary of ICI for years, but had never actually endorsed the products before. What used to happen was that Percy would give talks sponsored by ICI, at which the products would be prominently displayed, but he would not actually refer to them.

When he was asked to make the commercials, his daughter Margaret recalled recently, he asked the BBC for permission and since he didn't hear back, assumed that it was all right and went ahead. It wasn't all right, however, and he was sacked. The rules about television presenters promoting products were much stricter then and, although Percy had been able to work with ICI and even, in 1970, open Percy Thrower's Gardening Centre in Shrewsbury, the BBC felt that these commercials were a step too far because they could be seen as compromising the independence of the horticultural advice he gave on *Gardeners' World*. As Peter Seabrook pointed out, viewers could watch Percy at The Magnolias on BBC2 feeding his roses, then switch over to ITV and see a commercial with Arthur at The Magnolias feeding his roses with ICI's Rose Plus.

Barrie Edgar was very sad to see Percy go, not just because he liked him personally, but because he was such a joy to work with. 'We used to record the programmes in order on videotape, so that towards the end we would know exactly how much time we had left for the final item. I would ask the floor manager to tell Percy we had 3 minutes 29 seconds and Percy would be out in 3 minutes 28 seconds. We never had to edit him at all.' And all without a script. After his initial broadcasting experiences on radio, where he found it very difficult to work from a script – even one he had written himself – he always ad libbed. He turned out to be a skilled performer, something he never lost. The year before Percy died, the programme made a return visit to The Magnolias and decided to reprise a famous joke that had been played on Percy in the 'live' days of *Gardening Club*. Then, he would always walk into the greenhouse, take off his jacket and hang it on a nail. One day, the crew replaced the nail with a rubber one so that it bent and the jacket just slid off. Percy picked it up, thinking he hadn't put it on properly, put it back on the nail, and of course it slid off again. Finally, realising something was up, he just picked the jacket up and laid it on the bench.

'In 1987, the crew once again replaced the nail in the greenhouse with a rubber one,' recalled Dennis Gartside, producer at the time, 'and of course the jacket slid off. Percy handled it beautifully, but then we found, due to a technical fault, we hadn't recorded it so we needed to do it again. So we did and Percy's performance was so good no one ever knew it was the second time around.'

In 1976, with Percy gone, Clack's Farm became the programme's only base and Peter Seabrook, already known to viewers from *Dig This* and *Pebble Mill at One* was hastily brought in to join Arthur Billitt as the main presenter. 'The relationship between us was very different to the one Arthur had had with Percy,' Peter Seabrook remembered. 'They were contemporaries and old friends. With us, Arthur was the older experienced gardener who knew it all and I was the young lad who knew nothing !'

The two of them recorded two programmes in a day at Clack's Farm and two weeks later Peter recorded two programmes from a large garden somewhere in the UK.

Although Peter had done television before he had never presented directly to camera. 'The first location shoot I did was from the Ness Botanic Gardens in the Wirral. Because the cameras then were so big and heavy and could not be easily moved once they were in position, I wound up standing on a lawn talking to a camera that was about 100 yards away, which was unnerving to say the least.'

When John Kenyon became the programme's producer in 1979, he felt that Clack's Farm, although ideal for television in many ways – indeed it had been built for it – was too large and too perfect for many viewers to relate to.

'The night before we recorded a programme, I would wander round the garden with Arthur and, not being a gardener myself, I would ask why a plant wasn't doing too well. I wanted to know why and felt that viewers would want to know as well. So I'd say, "Let's do something about it on the programme tomorrow." But when tomorrow came, the sick plant had gone and something healthy would be in its place because, as I learnt, Arthur never had failures.'

He was also aware that Arthur Billitt wasn't getting any younger – he was in his late seventies. His fear was that if he suddenly had to retire through ill-health, they would lose the programme's base as well as a key presenter. So he started looking for a new presenter with a garden that could eventually take on that role. He talked to Alan Titchmarsh, then appearing on *Nationwide*, but felt that while he was clearly very talented, his garden in Hampshire was too far from Birmingham where the production team was based. It was also too far south which meant that, horticulturally speaking, everything happened in Alan's garden a week to four weeks earlier than in other parts of the country, so that the programme would be out of step with most of its audience.

At the end of 1979, however, since Peter Seabrook felt strongly that agriculture and horticulture do not mix, and John Kenyon was also in charge of the BBC's farming output, he made it clear he would leave *Gardeners' World*. The visiting experts, Clay Jones and Geoffrey Smith, were brought in as main presenters. But, although they were both passionately keen gardeners, their gardens

Above: Barrie Edgar with Arthur Billitt and Peter Seabrook.

in North Wales and Harrogate respectively were too far from Birmingham to be practicable as new bases for the programme.

Then John Kenyon met Geoff Hamilton, the editor of the monthly magazine *Practical Gardening*, through journalist Graham Rose, who was a mutual friend. He was sufficiently intrigued by Geoff's tales of the trial grounds he had developed for the magazine, and especially the garden he was about to develop from an overgrown piece of land around his home near Oakham in Rutland, to go and have a look. Although he says now that it was full of weeds and rubbish and that he had been conned, he felt the story of turning the wilderness into a garden – a situation that many gardeners are faced with – would make great television. What's more, it could hardly be in sharper contrast to the immaculate beds and borders of Clacks Farm. He also realised Geoff Hamilton's potential as a presenter, and saw in him a break with the past. Percy and Arthur had been gardeners of the old school, in Percy's case trained on big private estates and in public parks, and always gardened in a collar and tie. Kenyon like the fact that Geoff wore sweatshirts and jeans, usually with muddy knees, and

that he shared his own view of what gardening programmes should be like – dirty-handed, down-to-earth and practical.

The first programme from Barnsdale, as they decided to call the site, went out on the 21st March 1980 with Clay Jones and Geoffrey Smith as the main presenters since Geoff had only had a little broadcasting experience on Anglia TV's *Gardening Diary* some years earlier. Clack's Farm continued to be the show's main base, with Arthur Billitt and usually Geoffrey Smith, while Clay was the main presenter from Barnsdale as well as on location. Over the next two years, Barnsdale featured more and more and, by the end of 1981, when Arthur Billitt finally retired, it had become *Gardeners' World's* main base.

Geoffrey Smith decided that with *Gardeners' Question Time*, *Gardeners' Direct Line* and a major new television series of his own to make – *Geoffrey Smith's World of Flowers* – he no longer had the time to be a regular presenter on the programme. So Clay Jones took on the lead role with Geoff Hamilton doing more and more as his confidence as a broadcaster grew.

The very last *Gardeners' World* that Geoffrey Smith presented in 1982 featured the country's leading plantsman, Roy Lancaster, who soon became a regular member of the team. The same year saw the programme's first-ever female presenter join the team – Mary Spiller, an experienced plantswoman from the famous Waterperry Gardens in Wheatley, near Oxford. With Geoff now as the main presenter, the tone of the programme changed. Although he was horticulturally qualified and vastly experienced, his approach wasn't that of a teacher. It was that of a fellow gardener, sharing ideas, tips and experiences. Initially Geoff was reluctant to share failures, but when he and Clay pulled back a sheet of black polythene to show the seeds that should have germinated underneath but found only a forest of weeds, John Kenyon had it all on tape and insisted, against Geoff's wishes, that it was transmitted. Viewers were so encouraged by the fact that even someone like Geoff had failures that, from then on, he always shared them with the viewers just as he shared his triumphs.

The following year, it became clear that the two acres at Barnsdale were no longer big enough for the programme's needs, and as Geoff was only renting, he was understandably reluctant to invest more money in it. Towards the end of 1983, a Victorian house with outbuildings and five acres of virgin farmland, about a mile from Barnsdale, came on the market and Geoff bought it.

Many plants made the journey from Barnsdale Mark 1 to Barnsdale Mark 2 – it was decided to keep the same name for the new garden to avoid confusion – and some mature trees were planted to create some instant height in what was otherwise a completely flat site. These activities were filmed and the first programme in 1984, featured Geoff, Roy, Clay and new presenter Anne Mayo replanting the translocated plants in their new homes.

Over the next twelve years, Barnsdale became the ideal outdoor television studio, with each series seeing the creation of another new small garden – something to

which the majority of viewers who also had small gardens could easily relate.

Until 1990 the format remained the same – one week the programme came from Barnsdale with the presenters all working in the garden, and the following week, or sometimes the following two weeks, it came from a large garden somewhere in the UK. Although the technology was getting smaller and lighter, and it would have been possible to film in smaller gardens than before, budgetary considerations

Early days at Barnsdale Mark 2, as Geoff plants some trees.

ABOVE: Clay Jones, producer John Kenyon, centre, and Geoff watch Adrian Bloom do all the work.

meant that any garden chosen had be large enough to sustain a whole programme.

Although the vans.had become smaller, the programmes were still shot as outside broadcasts, with cameras still linked by cables to the scanner. The programmes continued to be recorded on to videotape in order, so that by the end of the two-day shoot, the team would leave with finished programmes, ready for transmission.

Presenters came and went – journalist Graham Rose, the man who had first introduced Geoff to John Kenyon some years before, Margaret Waddy, John Kelly, Nigel Colborn, Anne Swithinbank, Pippa Greenwood, and Dr Stefan Buczacki.

In 1990, the format changed. Instead of filming whole programmes in one location, *Gardeners' World* became a magazine programme. Barnsdale was the base each week, and Geoff doing practical tasks formed the spine of the programme, linking a series of pre-filmed items from different locations, some of which he also presented while the other presenters did the rest. In many ways, the changes made the programme more realistic. For one thing, Geoff was now gardening in his own garden alone,

not with two or three other people sharing the work, which is of course how the vast majority of people garden.

The other major change was a technical one. The programme was no longer shot as an outside broadcast, but shot on PSC – Portable Single Camera. Instead of several cameras cabled up to a scanner, there was one handheld camera recording direct to videotape in the camera itself. Whereas before three cameras would film an activity simultaneously in real time – in close up, in mid shot and in long shot – with the director choosing best shot, it now had to be done three times for the camera.

This means that the presenters have to become more like performers, able to repeat what they've done and said three times, as close to the original as possible. And this is where the production assistants who are responsible for continuity are worth their weight in gold. They will have noted in which hand the pot was first picked up, or which finger was used to touch a leaf. A presenter might be sure he or she had done something with their right hand, because doing it with the left feels so awkward but yet, when the tape is run back to check (something that is done as rarely as possible because the quality of the tape can be affected), it shows that they did use their left.

ABOVE: 'Versailles' – the first area to be developed at Barnsdale Mark 2.

When the presenter is talking about particular plants, a note is made and afterwards, the cameraman will film lingering close-ups of those plants, which are then edited into the finished sequence at the relevant point. The development of macro lenses mean that it's possible to get huge, mouth-watering close-ups of plants. Interviews are done in a similar way. They will be shot first of all with the camera on the guest, then some parts of the interview will be shot again, as a 'two-shot', with both guest and presenter. Finally, the 'cut aways' will be shot – close-ups of the presenter asking the questions and reacting to the answers by smiling or nodding encouragingly. These 'noddies' are invaluable in editing when it comes to shortening an answer. If a chunk of an answer were to be simply cut out of the middle, there would be a very obvious jump but, by cutting to a shot of the presenter listening to bridge the gap, that is avoided. The presenter needs someone to look at, so that his or her eye line is correct and will match that in the 'two shot'.

Sometimes, the guest will stay for the 'noddies', but it's not necessary since he or she is not in the shot, so sometimes a member of the production team will stand in. And sometimes this creates problems of its own. There was one famous occasion when Geoff Hamilton was filming a story on orchids in Costa Rica and got the giggles, prompted, he claimed, by the director's sun visor, and attempt after attempt ended in gales of helpless laughter.

With the small lightweight cameras and the magazine format, which meant that items needed to last only six or seven minutes, it became possible to film in much smaller gardens, the sort of gardens that the vast majority of the audience have. While the technical crew became much smaller – one cameraman and a sound recordist – the production team became much larger. With each programme containing three or four filmed items from different locations, sometimes hundreds of miles apart, more researchers and directors were needed. Another advantage of the magazine format was that in February and March, when the weather was often grim and no garden was looking its best, viewers could be inspired by beautiful plants and gardens shot the previous summer.

At the same time, however, the editorial direction of *Gardeners' World* moved away from dirty-handed, practical gardening, which had always been at the heart of the programme, towards lifestyle and leisure in an attempt to woo viewers who were not gardeners, and the audience began to dwindle as a result.

When an independent production company, Catalyst Television, took over in 1992, as a result of the government's insistence on the BBC accepting a 25 per cent quota of independently made programmes, practical gardening again became the priority. Garden writer Stephan Lacey and agricultural journalist-turned-garden designer Liz Rigbey joined Geoff and Pippa Greenwood and the audience soon returned.

By 1996, Geoff Hamilton felt that, after sixteen years, it was time to move on. He had also been asked to make a series for BBC 1 – *Geoff Hamilton's Gardening Week*, and his unfulfilled ambition was to see gardening on the majority channel with its much larger potential audience. Having suffered a heart attack the previous year, he also wanted to ease his workload a bit, and he felt that just working in his own garden on routine gardening tasks would be less demanding.

Alan found himself taking over some six months earlier than planned and in difficult circumstances, having lost a very good friend.

The format remained the same for the next four years – Alan gardening at Barleywood, as his garden was named just minutes before the *Radio Times* went to press, was the spine of the programme. Of course the programme changed – Geoff and Alan have different personalities and priorities. Geoff loved a bargain and knocking things up for 'a couple of bob' gave him enormous satisfaction. Alan has perhaps a more strongly developed aesthetic sense than Geoff and simply would not entertain anything made from wire coat hangers and polythene from the dry cleaning in his garden. When Geoff started, Barnsdale was a blank canvas, on the flat, so it was very easy to create a series of small demonstration gardens especially for television. When Alan started, Barleywood was already a very well-

ABOVE: The Mediterranean garden at Barleywood.

The obvious successor was Alan Titchmarsh, as experienced a broadcaster as he was a gardener. Although his garden was still in Hampshire, there was no longer a huge outside broadcast unit to transport to the location each week, so that wasn't a problem. And with the prerecorded items coming from all over the British Isles each week, the programme would reflect the differences in climate that gardeners faced.

The plan was that Geoff would launch the new series in February 1997 then, at Easter, hand over to Alan. Sadly though, Geoff died of a heart attack in August 1996, and

established garden with limited space and on a very steep slope, so that wasn't an option. Television changed too; direction became pacier, items shorter, and though some viewers disliked the changes, earlier programmes seem very slow when viewed now.

As ever, presenters came and went – Stephan Lacey and Pippa Greenwood were joined by Nick Wray, Vanessa Collingridge, Gay Search, Valerie Waters, Ivan Hicks – with some staying longer than others. Advertisements in the gardening press for new young talent in the late 1990s produced Rachel de Thame and Joe Swift.

LEFT: The start of the slope at Barleywood.

ABOVE: *Gardeners' World*'s new home – Berryfields – in winter.

In 2000, the format changed yet again. It was back to the early days of the programme with the presenters – a young team of Rachel and Joe joined by Chris Beardshaw, replacing the old guard – all working with Alan in his garden. There were fewer visits to other people's gardens.

In 2002, Alan decided that seven years on *Gardeners' World* was enough and he didn't want to become bored or boring. Besides he had been offered two exciting new projects – a history of Royal gardens and a major series on the natural history of the British Isles – and there were not enough days in the week to do it all.

Coincidentally, he was about to move house and having shared his garden for many years first with *Breakfast Time* and then *Gardeners' World* viewers, he wanted the new garden he would be creating to be a camera-free zone,

just for him, his family and his friends. This time there was no obvious successor, no one with Alan's depth of horticultural experience and knowledge combined with his consummate skills as a broadcaster. Several high profile names and an unknown or two were considered and, in the end, Monty Don, *The Observer*'s gardening columnist and presenter of various Channel 4 gardening programmes, was chosen as the main presenter, with Rachel de Thame and Chris Beardshaw in support.

The BBC took the programme back in house and for the first time since the very early days the base is not the main presenter's own garden. Instead, the BBC has leased a large private garden in the West Midlands, which will be developed over time . As ever presenters have come and gone, but *Gardeners' World* remains the one authoritative repository of practical horticulture on television and in Monty, a man who is never happier than when he has dirt under his fingernails, at the helm, it is clearly in safe hands.

Presenter 1969 – 1976

Percy Thrower

Percy Thrower's one ambition from earliest childhood was to be a head gardener like his father, Harry. Born in 1913 on the estate where his father worked, Horwood House in Buckinghamshire, Percy started helping his father and cultivating his own small patch of garden from very early on.

In 1931, Percy went to work as an improver – the stage between garden boy and journeyman – in the royal gardens at Windsor, working mainly in the huge glasshouses. He also met and secretly courted Connie, the daughter of the head gardener, CH Cook (they were later married, days after the outbreak of the Second World War in 1939). In 1935 Percy decided to move on for, with some sixty other gardeners there, promotion was hard to come by. Private service was already in decline, so he decided to try the public sector – parks departments. After two years with Leeds City Council, he moved to Derby

in 1937, working his way up to assistant parks superintendent. When war broke out, he became actively involved in growing food in the parks and also in the Dig for Victory campaign, showing how people could grow produce in their back gardens. Percy tried to enlist twice but was turned down on the grounds that the war work he was doing was far more useful.

When he took the job of parks superintendent in Shrewsbury on 1 January 1946, he was, at thirty-three, the youngest parks superintendent in the country. He was to stay there until his retirement over thirty years later. That same year, he made his first radio broadcast, being interviewed on *Round and About* about the Shrewsbury floral festival. A couple of years later, he was asked to appear on *Beyond the Back Door* which, in the spirit of Dig for Victory, included gardening along with raising chickens, rabbits and so on for food. He was invited to do a regular item on 'jobs for the month' on the first Sunday of every month from the studio in Birmingham. *Beyond the Back Door* gradually lost the livestock element and concentrated on gardening. It changed its name to *In Your Garden* and ran for many years.

His move into television came in 1951, when he was interviewed on a magazine programme called *Picture Page* about a British garden he had created in Berlin. That led to *Country Calendar*, on which he presented the gardening slots in all weathers from a garden specially adapted for television on a farm between Birmingham and Coventry.

Then came *Out and About* and *Gardening Club*, one strand of *Club Night*, which included *Smokers' Club*, *Inventors' Club* and even *Asian Club*. These soon fell by the wayside, but *Gardening Club* went from strength to strength. Its base became a studio in Gosta Green, Birmingham. Here there was a greenhouse with no glass so that there were no problems with reflections and the huge cameras could get right in close to see what Percy was doing. There was also a shed that was carted in and out every week too, along with a ton of topsoil and plants. By 1960 Percy was a household name. No wonder that ICI, then a leading manufacturer of garden products, was keen to be associated with him. Although he had no contract with the BBC, Percy was aware of its sensitivities about commercial interests and so did not advertise products directly, merely appearing at events organised by ICI at which their garden products would be on display.

It was through ICI that Percy became involved as a consultant to one of the very first garden centres to be set up in this country in 1967 – at Syon Park, west of London. Although the venture was not a runaway success, Percy recognised that this was the future and so, in 1970, he bought Murrells rose nursery in Shrewsbury and set up

Percy Thrower's Gardening Centre, which is still there today, run by his three daughters. He was also one of the first to spot the potential of gardening holidays and cruises and set up a travel company with two Shrewsbury travel agents. As well as gardening weekends in country hotels, he led trips to Europe and later to the Caribbean and South Africa.

Journalism followed television and Percy was soon writing first for *Amateur Gardening* and other magazines, then for national newspapers, including the *Sunday* and *Daily Express* and finally the *Daily Mail*.

In the early 1960s, although he was only just fifty, he decided to build a house for his retirement. Having always lived in tied accommodation, he and Connie had never owned a house. So on land he had originally bought for shooting, he built The Magnolias (see page 50) the garden of which was finished just in time for the start of *Gardeners' World* in 1968. For the first six years of the programme, Percy carried on with the day job. When he retired as parks superintendent in 1974, he also became the *Blue Peter* gardener, cultivating a small plot 3.6 x 3m (12 x 10ft) at the side of BBC Television Centre at White City.

In 1976, when Percy made the series of TV commercials for ICI gardening products, he was immediately dropped from *Gardeners' World*. 'Percy Throw-out', 'The BBC Throws out Thrower' and 'Percy Finds Himself in the Fertiliser' were typical newspaper headlines.

He stayed on as *Blue Peter*'s gardener until just before his death in March 1988, even managing to record a piece for the programme from the hospital just before he died. He made other television series, wrote many books and articles and carried on hosting gardening holidays and cruises.

Percy had an enormous impact on gardening. For many years after his death, Percy Thrower was still to gardening what Stirling Moss was to motor racing – almost the generic term. He continues to have an influence today through the Percy Thrower Bursary Trust, which offers a travel bursary each year to the student winner of the Young Horticulturalist of the Year.

The Nation's
Favourite Flowers

Lilies

It came as something of a surprise to learn, from all the votes cast by *Gardeners' World* viewers on the website and on the phone, that the nation's favourite flower is no longer the rose. It's the lily.

When you look at those beautiful, elegant trumpet flowers, though, it's easy to understand why. They look marvellous in borders or tubs and of course they are a superb cut flower – Number One on that list of the nation's favourites, too.

Most of them are powerfully fragrant. Interestingly, the fragrance is not produced by an essential oil so it cannot be extracted.

The main groups of trumpet lilies are the brightly coloured Asiatic hybrids, which are not usually scented; the Oriental hybrids, which have flowers in a range of colours, most of them scented; and the highly fragrant Longiflorum hybrids.

LOADS AND LOADS OF LILIES

Our appetite for lilies is almost insatiable. Derf Paton's nursery, near the New Forest, has three and a half acres of glasshouses devoted to producing lilies alone, and ships out a staggering hundred and ninety thousand pots of them each week to superstores and garden centres all over the country. For years, tall lilies were in demand, particularly by the cut-flower trade. But now, more compact varieties, ideal for growing on patios, are much more popular.

At the nursery, the lily bulbs are potted up by hand. Stem-rooting varieties need to be planted deep, so they put just a little of the rough, free-draining compost they use in the bottom of the pot. Next, they place three lily bulbs on it at a slight angle, with the tip facing out towards the sides of the pot. What happens is that when the shoots emerge, they hit the side of the pot and run straight up it giving you good straight stems, evenly spaced. The pots are then

filled with compost, and it's important not to firm it down but to leave it light and loose. They're given a good watering, then left for a week, and once the new growth is through, they are watered from above and fed with liquid feed right up to the time they are about to flower.

Once the lilies are in flower, Derf recommends pinching out the stamens, not so much to reduce the risk of the pollen staining as to prolong the life of each flower. Derf suggests that once the lilies have finished flowering you start feeding again with something like tomato fertiliser to build the bulbs up for flowering again next year.

OPPOSITE: *Lilium regale.*

Roses

Although beaten into second place by the upstart lily, the rose is still the favourite flower of many, not only for its colour, its form and its delicious scent, but for its romantic associations. Another huge genus, it ranges from exquisite miniatures only a few inches high to ramblers that can happily scramble 30m (100 ft) or more up a large tree.

Roses like rich, fertile soil that holds moisture but isn't boggy and, while many will cope with dappled shade, they do best in full sun. As with clematis , some people find the prospect of pruning daunting but it's not that complicated. As Geoff Hamilton found on a visit to the National Rose Society's gardens near St Albans in 1992, a trial showed that roses cut back with a hedge-trimmer flowered as freely than those pruned carefully in textbook fashion with secateurs. The bushes did look a bit of a mess, but the point Geoff made is that you really don't need to worry about getting it perfect.

ROSES AT HADDON HALL

Although the house at Haddon Hall, near Bakewell in Derbyshire, dates back to the 1680s, the gardens were laid out in the 1920s by the ninth Duchess of Rutland, a passionate rose lover. Tom Pope, who has been head gardener there for eighteen years, is keen to mix outstanding new roses with the older varieties to keep the garden alive and evolving. There's 'Eurostar' a vibrant yellow introduced in the late 1990s, as well as one of the very best new English roses bred by David Austin, the bright egg-yolk yellow Rosa GRAHAM THOMAS. Tom is especially fond of shrub roses such as 'Buff Beauty' and grows four plants together on a wooden framework, pulling the new long shoots horizontal and tying them down to encourage more side shoots and therefore freer flowering.

His favourites include 'Commandant Beaurepair', with its large, double crimson flowers, streaked pink and purple and marbled white; the very fragrant, rich scarlet 'James Mason'; the tall pillar rose with flowers of a similar colour DUBLIN BAY (syn. 'Macdub'); the tall, pink, richly scented L'AIMANT (syn. 'Harzola') and the Incense rose (Rosa primula), chosen unusually for its highly fragrant, fern-like foliage rather than its small, single, pale yellow flowers. 'I always recommend people to plant it because the fragrance fills the whole garden.'

ABOVE LEFT: *Rosa* GRAHAM THOMAS (syn. *R.* 'Ausmas').
LEFT: *Rosa* 'James Mason'.
OPPOSITE: *Rosa* GERTRUDE JEKYLL (syn. *R.* 'Ausbord').

Daffodils

No surprise that people love this harbinger of spring. As Michael Caine once said, when you see the first daffodil at the end of the winter, you bloomin' well feel you deserve it! They are very versatile. You can grow them in beds and borders, naturalised in grass, in pots, window boxes or even hanging baskets, and they are easy to grow.

As long as you leave the leaves alone for six weeks after flowering has finished – and this means not tying them in neat bunches either – feed them during this time, and divide the clump every few years, they will come up spring after spring. They like fertile, moist but not waterlogged soil and a sunny spot, though they are ideal for growing under deciduous trees because they have flowered before the leaves on the trees open and take all the light.

CORNISH DAFFODILS

Narcissi are in Ron Scamp's blood – his grandfather and his uncle were both commercial growers and though he works full time for a furniture chain, he's run his own business in Falmouth, Cornwall, along with his wife Maureen, breeding and supplying daffodil bulbs for the last fourteen years. He takes a great deal of trouble over new introductions, growing them on and keeping detailed records of how they perform for at least four years before

they are offered for sale. He has a superb split corona, or orchid-flowered, peach-pink variety, as yet not named, and a new golden egg-yolk yellow double, named 'Madam Speaker' after Dame Betty Boothroyd in her capacity as patron of the Marie Curie Cancer Care charity. Other new varieties have local rather than national connections. A delightful pure white triandrus hybrid was named 'Budock Bells' at the suggestion of members of the St Budock Women's Institute who had admired it in Ron's field in the parish while the bell ringers were practising in the church nearby.

'I defy anybody to say that this isn't the best of flowers,' said Ron, 'I can just about get by without daffodils for six or seven months, but then I get as much pleasure from lifting good healthy hard bulbs as I do from discovering a brand new seedling flower. No, I couldn't get by without daffodils.'

BELOW: *Narcissus* 'Madam Speaker'.

BELOW: *Narcissus* 'Budock Bells'.

OPPOSITE: *Narcissus* in dappled spring sun beneath deciduous trees.

Fuchsias

The fuchsia, the Barbara Cartland of the flower world, finished in the nation's favourites in fourth place. Though the fuchsia is named after the sixteenth century German herbalist, Leonhart Fuchs, he had nothing to do with its discovery. It was, in fact, discovered in the Dominican Republic in the late seventeenth century by Father Charles Plumier, a missionary and botanist who named the plant *Fuchsia triphylla flore coccinea* after Fuchs, whom he greatly admired.

It's a huge genus, with well over three thousand varieties on sale ranging from small-flowered hardy shrubs through extravagant hybrids with more frills than a line of can-can dancers, to small creeping species, with greenish yellow and orange flowers and purple sepals, bearing bright blue pollen, which even produces a small edible fruit. The flowers range from white through many shades of pink, to red and purple and even, with the slender-flowered triphylla varieties, bright orange. Grow them in borders, as hedges, in containers, window boxes or hanging baskets. They'll reward you with flowers from midsummer right through to autumn.

Not surprisingly, a group as big as the fuchsias attracts a fanatical following. Eric Coupland, from Carlisle, is one such passionate grower of fuchsias. His front garden is

BELOW: *Fuchsia* **'Thalia'.**

the first clue – it's full of hardy varieties that stay out all year round. 'At the back end of the year, I cut the tops off, to stop the wind waffing them a lot in the winter. Then in March I cut them down to their stocking tops – about three or four inches from the ground. Some might want them to grow into six-foot plants. In that case, you just leave more on.' In his back garden, he grows a range of tender hybrids, all in tubs set out on gravel.

Eric loves them because they are so versatile. 'You can grow them as standards, which is my favourite way, fans, balls, pillars, hoops.' He grows some of the most popular types, like the fully double blush white 'Annabel' and the generously large-flowered CHARLIE DIMMOCK (syn. 'Foncha') but he's also keen on more unusual species such as *F. paniculata*, whose flowers look exactly like racemes of lilac – hence its common name, the Lilac fuchsia.

While flowers are clearly the main attraction here, Eric also grows some for their foliage, 'Firecracker', for example, which has variegated leaves suffused with hot fuchsia pink. 'I've got eight or nine plants to a pot, and I've kept on stopping it [pinching out the growing tips to make it bushy]. I've had no flowers yet but they'll come. Anyway does it matter? People will look at that and think it's beautiful.'

OPPOSITE: *Fuchsia* **'Annabel'.**

Delphiniums

The delphinium, the nation's fifth favourite flower, is equally at home in a grand herbaceous border as in a cottage garden. The tall slender spikes of the Elatum hybrids can reach 2m (6ft) in height, while the Pacific hybrids are shorter and the flower spikes of the Belladonna hybrids are less densely packed.

They come in a whole range of colours – pink, red, cream and white, but the most popular shades are the whole range of blues, from palest sky through bright Gauloise to deep midnight. They add height and structure to any border and, while the flower spikes are dramatic and stunning, the individual flowers are equally beautiful. They also have very attractive bright green, deeply cut foliage.

For really small or exposed windy gardens, the much looser Grandiflorum type delphiniums, which carry their flowers individually on wiry stems, are more suitable.

WEDDING DAY DELPHINIUMS

Delphiniums are becoming a very popular wedding flower – not in the bridal bouquet but as confetti. Charles Hudson lives opposite an old church near Pershore in Worcestershire. One day, he had noticed a mass of paper confetti, looking dirty and messy on the road outside the church, and thought, Why not make confetti out of flower petals? Not only would they look wonderful but, they are completely biodegradable so they break down and disappear quickly, which meant that people could start using confetti in churchyards once again.

'So I started to experiment with different flowers – *Helichrysum*, poppies, *Nigella* – and found that annual delphiniums had a wonderful colour range and that, if dried naturally, the petals kept their shape and colour best.'

He started growing the flowers for confetti in his garden, then on an allotment in the village and now, as the business has expanded, it's a field-sized operation. The annual delphiniums are sown in succession, then the flowerheads are picked and hung upside down indoors, in good ventilation, to dry for about three weeks. Then they are ready for the next stage. 'Sifting and sorting takes a while because it's important to get rid of all the bugs and beetles and seed pods – the sort of things you really don't want to be throwing at the bride.'

BELOW: *Delphinium* 'Kestrel'.

OPPOSITE: *Delphinium* 'Sungleam'.

Clematis

One of the most versatile genera of all with literally thousands of cultivated forms, the clematis includes not only climbers, but also herbaceous and evergreen as well as deciduous types, with flowers for practically every day of the year, ranging from tiny bells to dessert-plate-sized blooms in colours from white to dark purple, including almost every colour of the rainbow in between.

The nation's sixth favourite flower is easy to grow: roots in shade, heads in sun, is a useful rule of thumb and they need plenty of moisture. Although some people are daunted by pruning, it's really not that complicated and some don't need pruning at all.

John and Ruth Gooch, of Thorncroft Nurseries near Norwich, are among the country's leading specialists with over three hundred different clematis in stock and, at the nurseries, they like to show visitors many different ways of growing clematis. 'Take the support away and they scramble,' said Ruth Gooch, 'for example, we have the dusky pink 'Margaret Hunt' scrambling over winter-flowering heathers, which adds a whole new dimension to gardening.' While some of the climbers scramble well, so do the non-clinging varieties, such as 'Rooguchi', a new Japanese cross between *C. integrifolia* and *C. reticulata*, which has exquisite, nodding, dark indigo-purple flowers and puts on over 2m (8ft) of growth each year.

If you want to grow clematis in pots, Ruth says, you need a good deep, thick-walled pot – terracotta is ideal – to keep the roots cool and allow for a good planting depth and then you must pay particular attention to feeding and watering. A tough species, such as the bright magenta-purple Polish-bred 'Kacper' (pronounced Casper) is ideal for a pot, and for slightly tender cultivars, such as the *C. florida* Pistachio, named for its central boss of pistachio-green stamens, container growing is ideal, allowing them to be moved into a cool conservatory or greenhouse for the winter.

For beginners, the Gooches recommend the small-flowered viticella hybrids, which are so easy to grow anywhere – up walls and fences, through other climbers or shrubs or scrambling over ground-cover plants. They are also the easiest to prune: simply cut them right back to the lowest pair of fat buds every spring.

BELOW: *Clematis* 'Rooguchi'.

BELOW: *Clematis florida* Pistachio (syn. 'Evirida').

OPPOSITE: *Clematis* 'Victoria'.

Sweet Peas

Surprising, perhaps, given how many people are passionate about sweet peas that they only came in seventh place. Many people grow them as the ideal, easy annual climber for colour on fences, up tripods or in tubs and, of course, for their wonderful scent, both outside and indoors as a cut flower.

For some years, in an attempt to get larger blooms and a wider range of colours, the breeders left scent out of the equation but now, due to popular demand, it's back and the varieties with the strongest perfume are the best sellers. They are not fussy about soil as long as it's not too wet or too dry, and do best in a sunny spot. Incidentally 'Percy Thrower', 'Geoff Hamilton' and 'Alan Titchmarsh' are all sweet peas.

SWEET PEAS AT DAWN

For many people, growing sweet peas just for their beauty isn't enough. For them, it's a competitive sport. *Gardeners' World* followed two competitors in the National Sweet Pea Show at Bosworth in Leicestershire in June 2002. Angie Gillespie was a first-timer at this level, while Alec Cave, an old hand, was setting his sights on the *Daily Mail* Cup, awarded for the best exhibit of twelve distinct varieties – one pink, one white, one lavender and so forth. What the judges look for in a prize-winning sweet pea is four blooms on a long straight stem, evenly spaced, with no stem showing between them and the blooms facing forward. As always, timing is absolutely crucial and since sweet peas are grown outside, unlike, say begonias, which are grown under glass, the weather is the clincher. Two days before the competition, in Angie Gillespie's part of the country, the heavens had opened. 'The weight of water is pulling the stems down,' she said. 'All you can do is shake the water off, and hope that maybe a bit of sun tomorrow will perk them up.'

Since judging starts at 7am, the competitors have to be up very early to put the finishing touches to their displays. 'At 3am,' said Alec Cave, 'the blooms are all screwed up, as though they are sleeping. As soon as dawn breaks, though, they wake up, start drinking and then start lifting.'

In the end Alec came second in the *Daily Mail* Cup but, as consolation, he won first prize in the lavender colour class.

OPPOSITE: *Lathyrus odoratus* '**Matucana**'.

Primulas

Primulas are another very large genus of over four hundred species that range from the modest soft yellow native primrose, *Primula vulgaris*, through the bright polyanthus hybrids and the astonishingly graphic auriculas, to the tall candelabra primulas and the dramatic giant cowslip, *P. florindae*, which reaches a good 1.2m (4ft) in height.

The main difference between primroses and polyanthus is that former have solitary flowers among the rosettes of leaves, while the latter, originally a cross between primroses and cowslips, carry theirs in loose heads on long stems held above the leaves. Primulas as a group have a very long flowering season from late winter to late summer. All primulas like some moisture. Some, like the auriculas, need the soil to be well drained too, while others, like the candelabra primulas, are ideal for bog gardens or pond margins. Some need full sun while most are happy in part shade or dappled woodland conditions.

HARLOW CARR'S PROMISCUOUS PRIMULAS

Primulas reproduce themselves by seed, but rather than keep themselves to themselves, they cross-pollinate very easily, producing masses of natural hybrids. At thc RHS northern garden near Harrogate, Harlow Carr, they have the most wonderfully vivid example of this promiscuous behaviour. There, two varieties of candelabra primulas – *P. bulleyana*, which has tightly packed whorls of orange and gold flowers, and *P. beesiana*, which has similar flowers in shades of cerise pink to purple – have crossed to produce Harlow Carr hybrids in some stunning colours. The fact that some have a white powdery coating, called meal, on their stems, suggest that yet another tall primula, *P. pulverulenta*, had a hand in their parentage (*pulverulenta* is the Latin for dusty, incidentally).

The bed was planted over fifty years ago when Harlow Carr belonged to the Northern Horticultural Society, and the fact that they have survived temperatures of minus eighteen degrees on wet clay is an indication of their hardiness. According to gardener, Alison Williams, they have a very long flowering period, from May to mid to late July, depending on the weather. The cooler it is, the longer they last.

ABOVE: *Primula* Harlow Carr hynrids
ABOVE LEFT: A fancy Florists' auricula.
OPPOSITE: Primrose, *Primula vulgaris*.

Poppies

There are many types of poppy all of which bring something different to the garden. The annual corn poppy, *Papaver rhoeas*, for example, has delicate, papery flowers in a range of colours from vibrant scarlet to the palest smoky lavender-grey. They are vulnerable to wind and sharp showers, which can quickly remove all the petals, but that only adds to their ephemeral charm.

Californian poppies, *Eschscholzia californica*, come in many colours, too, from the most brilliant orange and scarlet to cream. They are very easy to grow from seed, sown where they are to flower in free-draining soil, even in gravel, and in full sun.

The bigger Oriental poppies bring a much less innocent, blowsy decadence to the flower garden, with bold, jagged architectural foliage and their large flowers opening like so many scrumpled handfuls of tissue paper from bristly, pale green buds. When the flowers die, the show is not over because they are followed by handsome sculptural seed capsules. Oriental poppies like full sun and a well-drained soil, so heavy soils need the addition of grit to improve drainage. They have a large tap root which means that they can withstand drought well.

PATTY'S PLUM

Most Oriental poppies are in bright scarlet, orange or white, so it's no surprise that *Papaver orientale* 'Patty's Plum', with petals in a wonderfully smoky, purplish pink, the colour of damson fool, should have been such a huge hit since its introduction in the late 1990s.

Ironically, it was discovered in the garden of a celebrated nurserywoman, Patricia Morrow, along with a number of other seedlings that she considered far more beautiful than this rather dull and muddy specimen. She was all for consigning it to the compost heap, but fortunately Sandra and Nori Pope, of Hadspen Gardens, were visiting her at the time and, since they leapt to its defence, she told them to dig it up and take it away. They did, eagerly, since they saw what a valuable addition to the gardener's pallet this marvellous colour would be. They named it after her – it's 'Patty's Plum' though, not 'Patricia's Plum'. She is delighted that it's been a success but still has her reservations. She admits it's lovely when it first opens, but says it fades a bit.

BELOW: *Papaver orientale* 'Patty's Plum'.
BOTTOM: *Papaver rhoeas.*

Irises

Named after the goddess who was the messenger of the gods and who had as her symbol the rainbow, the irises bear flowers in every colour of the spectrum.

The irises range from small bulbs such as the dwarf *I. reticulata*, the rich velvety blue flowers of which open in winter, through to the delicate, butterfly-like flowers of *I. sibirica* and the large flamboyant flowers of the tall bearded irises. The latter used to be called 'fleur-de-lys' and, in profile, with the upright central 'standard' and two of the three arching 'falls' on either side, the shape, the symbol of pre-revolutionary France, is easily recognisable. Tenth on the list of the nation's favourite flowers, irises are easy to grow and are attacked by very few pests and diseases . A few, such as the flag iris, *I. pseudacorus*, and water iris, *I. laevigata*, like really moist soil as found at the margins of ponds, and *I. sibirica* and winter-flowering *I. unguicularis* prefer light shade, but the rest need well-drained soil and full sun. Although they can be grown in mixed borders, they do need to be planted where their rhizome can be baked by the sun to ensure good flowering the following year. They should be divided up every three or four years to ensure best flowering, and the ideal time is a few weeks after flowering is over.

IRIS FIELDS

Michael Loftus of Wootten Plants, near Southwold in Suffolk, is absolutely wild about irises. He now has over twelve acres of plants in cultivation, with over two hundred different varieties, and he loves hearing the Oohs and Ahhs of the visitors who come to visit the iris fields in June.

'Planting an iris field is like putting on a pantomime – it's like having so many dames all outdoing each other and each one more outrageous than the last.' Michael's own garden is shady so the only way he could grow these beautiful flamboyant plants was, he says, to buy a ten-acre field and get on with it. 'Irises must have free drainage and the soil here is perfect for them. It's very light, so light that it just falls from my hand. The traditional way to grow them was in beds by themselves, as Gertrude Jekyll did. She grew them in rectangular beds in the middle of stone terraces, which gave great air circulation, lots of sun and were very easy to weed.'

Asking Michael to choose a favourite iris is like asking him to choose a favourite child, but he is very impressed by 'Local Colour', which has deep violet flowers with ruffled black-violet falls as well as vermilion beards. One of the great favourites with visitors is 'Black Tie Affair', which has a deepest purple standard with near-black falls and a black beard.'When the sun lights it from behind, it just glows.'

Michael points out that irises make a wonderfully dramatic cut flower, that many of them are deliciously scented and they are very easy to grow. 'A man who is not inspired by an iris must be tired of life.'

ABOVE: The golden 'beard' of a bearded iris.
OPPOSITE: *Iris* 'Pearly Dawn'.

LILIES

Geoff Hamilton

Lilies need deep rich, but well-drained soil. If yours is heavy clay, dig in plenty of bulky organic matter and lay the bulbs on their sides on a layer of coarse grit at the bottom of the planting hole.

Percy Thrower

They need a cool root run, so the lower parts of the stems should be shaded from strong sunshine by interplanting with herbaceous plants or low-growing shrubs.

Pippa Greenwood

Bulbs establish more quickly if you soak them in water for an hour or so before planting.

ROSES

Geoff Hamilton

To encourage the stooling habit [flowering shoots arising from below soil level], it's best to plant a few centimetres deeper than they grew in the nursery – you'll normally be able to see a soil mark on the plant as an indication.

Percy Thrower

All newly panted hybrid teas and floribundas being pruned for the first time should be cut back to within 15–23cm (6–9in) of the ground. This is important as an initial hard pruning encourages strong growth the first year. Standard roses are worked high up on the main stem of the stock, so all shoots below the head of branches are suckers and must be removed as soon as these are noticed.

DAFFODILS

Percy Thrower

When planting daffodils in pots, I like to put the bulbs in two layers with a layer of soil in between. The bulbs in the top layer are placed above the spaces between the bulbs in the bottom layer and in this way it is possible to grow more plants in the one pot.

Geoff Hamilton

Give them a boost by feeding as soon as the flowers fade using a fertiliser high in potash – a rose or tomato fertiliser.

Alan Titchmarsh

After flowering, tidy the blooms by all means, but let the leaves stay for at least six weeks to fuel the plants for next year's blooms.

FUCHSIAS

Percy Thrower

If standard fuchsis are required for planting out later on, 'tipping' [pinching out the top of each shoot when it has produced four to six pairs of leaves] delays flowering and also enables them to stand up to wind much better than if the shoots were allowed to grow long without being stopped.

Geoff Hamilton

If you have kept tender fuchsias over the winter, start them into growth in March by standing the pot in water for a few minutes and prune back the twiggy top growth quite hard. Then knock the plant out of its pot and carefully scrape away as much old compost as possible from between the roots before returning it to the pot with some fresh compost.

DELPHINIUMS

Geoff Hamilton

Delphiniums can be sheared off right down to the crown, just above ground level. If you leave them, the foliage will collapse and swamp other smaller plants around them. Give the plants a sprinkling of fertiliser and a good soak of water and they'll soon produce fresh young leaves.

Arthur Billitt

Make sure that slugs are dealt with before the winter, otherwise they feed on the underground buds, which could even result in the death of the plant.

Percy Thrower

These will grow well from young shoots cut off below ground level in April. With delphiniums (and lupins), it is particularly important to get well down because higher up the growth is hollow and will not root easily.

CLEMATIS

Geoff Hamilton
Plant clematis so that the top of the rootball is about 15cm (6in) below soil level in case it iis attacked by clematis wilt. It will then produce healthy new growth from below soil level.

Percy Thrower
As clematis always appreciate a cool root run, try to arrange for the roots to be shaded by low-growing shrubs or large flat pebbles.

SWEET PEAS

Geoff Hamilton
For prize-winning blooms, never grow the main shoots up the canes as they quickly run out of steam and become 'blind'. Instead, tie the strongest side shoot from each plant to its cane and remove all others. Pinch out all subsequent side shoots and tendrils in order to direct all the plant's energy into the flowers. If the seeds are black and mottled, it's often best to soak them overnight first. Those that haven't swollen next morning can be 'snipped' by removing a tiny bit of the seed coat with a sharp knife.

Percy Thrower
In January, pot up autumn-sown sweet peas individually into 8cm (3in) pots of John Innes No 1. Place twiggy sticks around the edge of the pot to give the young plants the support they need.

PRIMULAS

Percy Thrower
In late May, it is a good idea to put a small stick against the best polyanthus so that, after flowering has finished, they may be lifted and divided. This splitting up is usually done in about the middle of June but, of course, the plants must be marked when they are at their best.

Pippa Greenwood
Primula seed is best sown fresh as soon as it has ripened.

Geoff Hamilton
Sow polyanthus on the surface of very moist, soilless compost and cover with the little vermiculite. Put clear polythene over the pots and keep them in full light as this is essential for germination.

POPPIES

Alan Titchmarsh
Stake oriental poppies early. If you leave it until they have flopped and then tie them up, they look like trussed-up turkeys.

Geoff Hamilton
Poppies hate to be disturbed so either sow them where they are to flower, or sow in modules under cover so that the young plants can be transplanted with no root disturbance. Once the Oriental poppies have finished flowering, their flopping foliage takes up a lot of valuable border space. Be ruthless and cut it right off down to the base. It will regrow and if you're lucky, you may benefit from another blooming in late summer.

IRISES

Alan Titchmarsh
With flag irises, [*Iris pseudacorus*] look for youthful bits around the edge of the clump, and cut off 3 to 4 inches of rhizome with roots behind. Bed two or three into aquatic compost in a basket, so that the rhizomes are almost on the surface, top dress with pea shingle and place on the margin of the pond.

Geoff Hamilton
Cut young laterals or side pieces, each with a fan of leaves, off the original old rhizome. Reduce the leaves on the young rhizomes by half their length and replant them in groups of three or four to make good-sized clumps. Make sure they are not completely buried, especially on heavier soil.

Arthur Billitt

Presenter 1969 – 1982

Born in March, Cambridgeshire, in 1902, all Arthur ever wanted to do was grow plants. Unfortunately his father had other ideas and, when Arthur left school, he was apprenticed to a local pharmacy. His dream of owning a piece of land remained, however, and eventually he saved up enough money to buy a small plot. A kindly local bulb grower helped him out by giving him bulbs and only expecting payment after Arthur had sold the resulting flowers.

In the early 1930s, the pharmacy was bought by Boots and, rather than become a pharmacist, Arthur suggested that they should develop an agricultural and horticultural division. Boots employed him to do a feasibility study and then, in 1935, to find a suitable place for a research station. Having moved to Nottingham, he eventually found the ideal site at Lenton House, the home of Boots chairman, Lord Trent. During the Second World War, Arthur, like Percy, was actively involved in the Dig for Victory campaign and set up demonstration allotments at Lenton. After the war, he devoted himself to research on pest, disease and weed control and plant nutrition.

Arthur had always been a long-term planner and so, in the mid 1950s, he set about looking for somewhere to which he could retire in fourteen years' time . His job had taken him all round the country and he decided that Herefordshire or Worcestershire was the place to be.

For him the most important factor wasn't location, location, location. It was soil, soil, soil. You could always change a house, he said, but you couldn't change the soil. Eventually, in 1955, he came across Clack's Farm near Droitwich, in Worcestershire, a rundown house with thirty-five acres of neglected land, and bought it (see page 54).

Arthur's broadcasting career had almost begun in 1938 when the famous radio gardener CH Middleton had asked him to take over his slot while he was on holiday. The BBC, however, had other ideas: Arthur was in commercial horticulture, which was unacceptable. Twelve years later he made his first radio broadcast – an interview about a new pesticide developed at Lenton. There followed some guest appearances with Percy on *In Your Garden* and then on *Gardening Club*. Between 1969 and 1975, Clack's Farm joined The Magnolias as a regular location for *Gardeners' World*. Then, following Percy's departure in 1976, it became the programme's main base.

By 1982, when Arthur was almost 80, the BBC decided that it was time to move on, and Barnsdale became the home of *Gardeners' World*. It wasn't quite the end of the road for Arthur or Clack's Farm though because it became the base for Central TV's regional programme *Gardening Time* until 1989 and Arthur continued to appear. He lived on in happy retirement, spending part of the year in New Zealand, until his death in 1992 at the age of ninety.

Peter Seabrook

Presenter 1976 – 1979

Brought up on his grandfather's farm, Peter's earliest ambition was go into horticulture, not agriculture. After studying at Writtle College, he worked in all aspects of commercial horticulture and was in at the start of the gardening revolution which saw the introduction of container-grown plants in 1963 and the development of garden centres. That year he started writing for *The Nurseryman and Seedman*, and has written for every issue since.

Peter's break into broadcasting came in the 1960s as a guest on *In Your Garden*. In 1970, he moved into television with Anglia's *Garden Diary*, where he and Geoff Hamilton crossed swords for the first but by no means the last time. The issue on this occasion was the relative merits of the new container-grown plants, which he supported, and traditional, bare-rooted plants, which Geoff preferred.

Dig This, from BBC's Pebble Mill studios in Birmingham, followed, but when that fell victim to the miner's strike as afternoon programmes were cancelled, Peter started to do regular gardening slots in the studio on *Pebble Mill at One*.

When Percy Thrower was sacked from *Gardeners' World* in 1976, Peter was asked to take over at very short notice. 'I was actually out with the producer doing the recce for my first garden visit when the news about Percy being sacked broke. My wife Margaret had asked me before I left

what would happen when the news broke, and I said "Oh, nothing. They won't be interested in me." But then I got a panic phone call from Margaret to say that Fleet Street had descended on our house and there was a man from the *Daily Express* trying to get into the bedroom.'

Peter appeared with Arthur at Clack's Farm and presented the programmes from other locations by himself, for which he was paid £75 per programme – a fee which included not only presenting but researching, advising and handling correspondence.

After he left *Gardeners' World* at the end of 1979, Peter carried on on television here and abroad, notably in the American gardening series *The Victory Garden*, which took him all over the world. He's been the gardening editor of *The Sun* for twenty-six years and, though he is no longer professionally involved in commercial horticulture, he is still very supportive of, and hugely knowledgeable about, every aspect of the industry.

'In my last ever *Gardeners' World*, there was a bit of role reversal. For an item about making a stone trough from an old butler's sink coated in sand, cement and peat, Jean Laughton, the producer's assistant, was the director, Barrie Edgar was the presenter and I was the producer. I always thought people behind the camera should try their hand in front of it, so that they would be a little more sympathetic!'

Gardeners' World
Base Gardens

The Magnolias

Percy Thrower had been an excellent shot all his life and shooting was always a favourite hobby, so in the late 1950 he bought some land to the north west of Shrewsbury specifically for shooting. He was up there one day with some friends, and realised what a fantastic view it had over the Shropshire landscape.

On a clear day you could for see sixty miles. It was then that Percy decided that this was a great spot to build a house. All his working life he had lived in tied accommodation, whether it was the bothy at Windsor or at Quarry Lodge, the large half-timbered park superintendent's house in Shrewsbury. Although his retirement was some years away, it made sense to plan ahead to the time when he and Connie would need a home of their own.

The site was challenging. It was 180m (600ft) above sea level, and the soil, usefully as it turned out for television gardening purposes, varied from gravelly at the top, medium loam half way down and heavy clay that was often waterlogged at the bottom, so covering on one site the main types of soil that viewers might have.

The Throwers designed the house themselves – a simple chalet bungalow built near the top of the slope to take full advantage of the view, with the principle rooms facing south over what would be the garden for the same reason. While the house was being built during 1962–63 Percy had planned to make a start on the garden – roughly one and half acres in size – but in the winter of '63 there was snow on the ground from New Year to Easter, so it was not possible. Strange though it may seem, given Percy's horticultural pre-eminence, he had never designed a garden from scratch before. He knew it had to be informal to fit into the surrounding countryside, because, laid out on the slope, the garden would be visible from outside, so there were to be no straight lines anywhere. Instead there were irregularly shaped, curving island beds throughout the garden, planted with trees

and shrubs. Percy had as much summer bedding at work as anyone could wish for so, apart from a couple of areas near the house, it had no place in his own garden. He was also thinking ahead to retirement when he would not be so active, and therefore the planting was designed to be low-maintenance.

Percy loved trees and planted nearly fifty including a Cedar of Lebanon (*Cedrus libani*) , a tulip tree (*Liriodendron tulipifera*), a dawn redwood (*Metasequoia glyptostroboides*) and no less than ten flowering cherries.

There were also a number of magnolias, although the garden was not named for them. In fact it was the other way round. As soon as he started to make the garden, Percy had asked the readers of *Amateur Gardening* to suggest a name. Flower names were the most popular, with magnolias somewhat surprisingly perhaps, at the top of the list. So 'The Magnolias' it became. Percy planted a number of his favourite varieties and fortunately the conditions suited them very well so that they thrived.

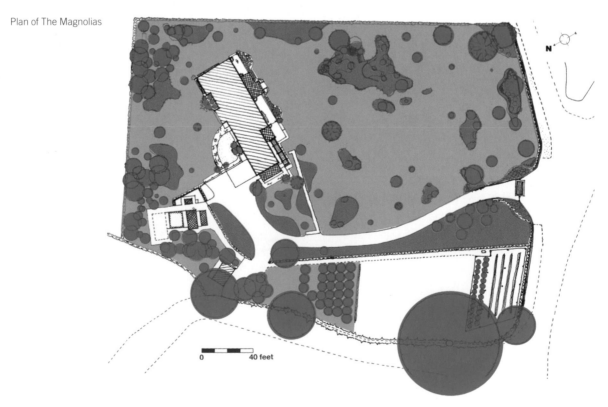

Plan of The Magnolias

0　　　　　40 feet

He planted hedges of hawthorn, beech and Leyland cypress around the garden and within it, and although Percy was then doing the studio-based *Gardening Club* on television, he planned the garden with television in mind, laying wide, hard paths for the cameras. Even so, The Magnolias was far from ideal for television in many ways. It was on such a steep slope that the cameras had to be propped up sometimes to keep them level, or platforms had to be built specially for them .

Percy loved lawn – with modern herbicides and mowers he felt it was no longer the labour-intensive chore to look after that it had been in his early days. But he sowed new lawn from seed only around the house. The rest was the original field grass, cut regularly to give fine grasses a chance to get established.

As for features, one of the first to be built was two linked rock-pools near the top of the slope in front of the house. These were fed with water collected from the roof, which was circulated by an electric pump. One important tip Percy passed on to people who were creating new gardens was to have ducts put in during the building work so that power and water could then easily be laid on to various points in the garden. Retaining walls were then built around the pools, large pieces of rock added, along with colourful alpines that provided colour and interest for a large part of the year.

Along the front of the house, Percy built a pergola – something he felt always had an old-world charm – which was smothered in climbing roses, clematis and honeysuckle. The uprights for the pergola were inserted into sections of drainpipe sunk into the ground so that when the wood eventually rotted, it would be comparatively easy to replace them.

On the west side of the garden was the fruit and vegetable plot, and in the far north-western corner, behind the house were four greenhouses – one which later had removable sides to allow the cameras access. Once his garden centre was up and running, many of Percy's tender plants were overwintered in the large greenhouses there.

It was, he felt , important not to rush at making a brand new garden, and he allowed himself eight years to develop The Magnolias fully, but in fact he completed it in four – just in time, as it turned out, for *Gardeners' World*! With a full time job, and broadcasting commitments that took him all over the country, Percy did not have time to care for the garden by himself. Connie, their three daughters, and later their husbands were roped in to help, and then he did take on a gardener, Sam Evans, to do the routine maintenance. Percy was also a great believer in modern chemicals. He used paraquat to keep the garden weed-free and was happy to use chemicals against pests and diseases. As far as Percy was concerned, DDT and BHC were far less dangerous than the lead, arsenic and nicotine that were used to spray against pests when he was a boy.

It wasn't just viewers of *Gardeners' World* who came to know The Magnolias well. From 1966 onwards, Percy held open days for charity, which attracted up to 10,000 visitors, with local farmers kindly allowing their fields to be used as car parks. Surprisingly, there was never any real damage to the garden. The grass took a bashing from thousands of pairs of feet, but it soon recovered and there was never any vandalism or theft.

The open days continued after Percy left *Gardeners' World* in 1975, and briefly after his death in 1988. His widow Connie still lives there, but she is now in her late eighties and not surprisingly, cannot keep the garden as it was in its prime.

Clack's Farm

When Arthur Billitt bought Clack's Farm near Droitwich in 1956,
the idea that it would one day become a television garden could
not have been further from his mind.

He had been looking for a place to which he could eventually retire and, having travelled the country as part of his work, had decided that Worcestershire was the place with the best soil. He was also looking for another place where his daughter Margaret, who had just left agricultural college, could set up a poultry farm. Clack's Farm, at first sight, was not promising. There was a near-derelict house, masses of rusty old farm machinery and thirty-five acres of overgrown wilderness. His wife, Gladys, took one look at the house and fainted, but the soil was good – reddish, light to medium loam over old red sandstone – and that's what mattered to Arthur. He took many soil samples and had them analysed. The soil was very low in nutrients, mainly because it had been over-farmed during the war years, but it could easily be made fertile again. He had the water supply thoroughly tested too, and that was declared 'potable', that is, suitable even for drinking. There was also plenty of room for Margaret's poultry venture.

So, he bought Clack's Farm in July 1956 for £5,200. Margaret moved in first and set up her poultry farm, while Arthur spent the next five years commuting over from Nottingham at weekends to clear the garden. Arthur never liked the name 'Clack's Farm', so he changed it very early on to Cherry Hill Farm. No mail arrived, though, and when he queried it with the postman, he was told firmly that he didn't know any 'Cherry Hill Farm', he only knew Clack's Farm, so that's what it remained.

In September 1968, the producer of *Gardeners' World*, Bill Duncalf, came to see him. He was looking for somewhere to create a large fruit and vegetable garden for the programme, around 500sq m (600sq yds). Although there was a fruit and vegetable plot at The Magnolias, the programme's current location, it was rather small and access to it was difficult. Could Arthur turn a patch of uncultivated land into a new kitchen garden, especially for television and be ready for filming at the start of the next series the following March?

Arthur agreed, although he realised that creating a fruit and vegetable garden in under six months, and mostly in winter would be no easy task. The layout was simple – two vegetable beds, a bed for soft fruit, standing ground for

pots and a small greenhouse. Between them, there were broad paths to accommodate the cameras. Arthur made good progress, in spite of the problem with the *Radio Times* announcing that apples, pears and plums would feature in the first programme. Arthur hadn't planned to include 'top' fruit in the garden so not only had he not planted any trees, there was nowhere to put them. Nothing daunted, Arthur moved the newly planted beech hedge that was to have been the vegetable garden's boundary and cleared another piece of wilderness. Within a week, the ground was ready for planting and, courtesy of an old nurseryman friend, the apples, pears and plums went in.

Plan of Clack's Farm

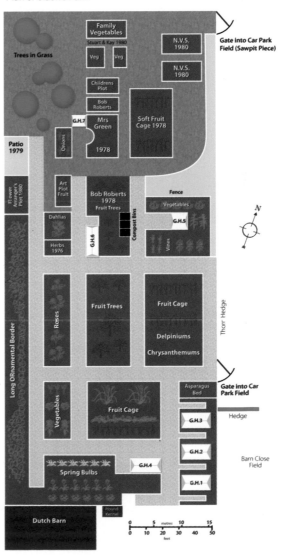

After the first two programmes were recorded, Arthur quickly learnt what gardening on television involved. The heavens had opened during the night turning the front garden into mud, so the huge BBC outside broadcast vehicles, parked there overnight, got bogged down and had to be towed out by tractor. The grass paths between the beds were churned to mud by the heavy camera dollies, so Arthur promptly laid paths of concrete slabs 1.2m (4ft) wide. Even they weren't wide enough – people had to step on to the beds to get past the cameras, which did the carefully prepared soil no good at all. So the width was doubled.

The fruit and vegetable garden at Clack's Farm was a major element *Gardeners' World* from 1969 to 1976. It expanded rapidly, almost doubling in size in the first two or three years, allowing more room for everything, including fruit that was not too common in those days, such as peaches and nectarines. Although Worcestershire, a great fruit-growing area, was renowned for bullfinches, which feasted on the fruit buds, Clack's Farm escaped unscathed for the first few years. But once word got out on the bullfinch grapevine, and bird scarers proved ineffective, there was no option but to put all the fruit trees

and bushes in fruit cages. One, and then two, more greenhouses were added, and an asparagus bed. In 1973, ornamental plants made their first appearance in the television garden, with a long shrub border along the western boundary. The following year saw the planting of the rose plot with hybrid teas, floribundas and climbing roses selected by the Royal National Rose Society.

After Percy Thrower's sudden departure from the programme and his replacement by Peter Seabrook in 1975, Clack's Farm became the main base. This meant that, in addition to the fruit and vegetables, it now had to accommodate the ornamental side of gardening too. So the television garden expanded by degrees to around 4,000sq m (about 4,800sq yds), and underwent many changes during those years.

In tune with the needs of the audience, there were many different small-scale plots. One of the most popular was Arthur's Plot, started in 1997. This was a patch 6 x 3m (20x 10ft) – something for which people with average-size gardens could find room – and the object was to see just how many vegetables he could produce on it. Arthur felt it was far too small, but agreed to give it a try and was surprised to find at the end of the first season that he had grown £65's worth of produce. The same year saw the creation of two children's plots, just 3 x 3m (10 x 10ft), cultivated under Dad's watchful eye by Peter Seabrook's children – Alison, who grew flowers, and Roger, who opted for vegetables.

The following year, 1978, Bob Roberts, who was blind, was invited to create his own vegetable garden. He was able to point out that the plot they had marked out for him

Producers and presenters past and present gather at Clack's Farm on 28th May 1980 to celebrate the 150th programme.

was an inch out of square and, what's more, to correct the angles before he started work. It was a very popular item, inspiring not only people who were blind or partially sighted, but also those with perfect vision.

In 1979, to reflect the increasing interest in outside living, a patio was created as a location for demonstrating the joys of container gardening. With the help of Dave Chapple, of the Midlands branch of the National Vegetable Society, another plot was developed for growing exhibition vegetables – giant leeks, monster runner beans and so on. This proved so popular that the following year, a new and larger plot was devoted to exhibition vegetables.

With John Kenyon now the producer, the patio had been used as a location for items by leading flower arranger Sheila McQueen. In 1980, she planted up a flower arranger's plot adjoining it to provide her raw materials, so that she didn't have hunt for them all over the garden. That year also saw development of the family vegetable garden. The Haywood family, friends of Arthur's, had recently moved into the area and, although neither Stuart nor Kay Haywood were experienced growers, they were keen to try to become self-sufficient in vegetables. They

were given a large plot of 63sq m (75sq yds), right opposite the exhibition vegetable plot, which might have been inspirational, or depressing, and by the end of the first season, they had come very close to their goal.

1980 also saw the transmission of the 150th edition of *Gardeners' World* on the 28th of May.'

In 1982, the BBC decided that Clacks Farm had outlived its usefulness as a location, and made Barnsdale the base for *Gardeners' World*. But Central Television stepped in the following year and it became the centre for their regional programme *Gardening Time* until 1989. When Arthur died in 1992, it was too big for his widow, Riet, to manage on her own, so Clack's Farm was sold in 1995.

Barnsdale

There were in fact two Barnsdales, both near Oakham in Rutland and both created with *Gardeners' World* in mind. In 1977, Geoff Hamilton was able to rent from an old friend a near-derelict cottage and two and a half acres of land on the Barnsdale Hall estate near Oakham.

He was then editor of *Practical Gardening*, as well as writing a weekly column for *Garden News*, and had turned some of the land into trial grounds for those publications. By the time he met producer John Kenyon in 1979, he had just moved into another cottage on the estate, in much better repair and closer to the trial grounds. The small area of garden that surrounded Top Cottage, as it was called, was full of brambles, nettles and other weeds, and it was the possibility of showing viewers how to turn such an unpromising site into a lovely garden, combined with the trial grounds, that finally sold John Kenyon on 'Barnsdale' as a base for *Gardeners' World*.

The garden, wrapped around Top Cottage, was the size of many suburban or new estate gardens, and became an early prototype of Geoff's modern cottage-garden style. There were generous beds with mixed planting; trees, shrubs, perennials and, in the first couple of years, masses of cheap and cheerful annuals. There were features too, such as a scree garden, a semicircle of paving planted with alpines, a woodland garden, even a heather and conifer bed (very early 1980s) and a generous amount of lawn in flowing curves around the house. The making of the garden featured in the programme during 1980 and 1981 and the following year featured in a book, *Gardeners' World Cottage Gardens*.

Over on the trial grounds, Geoff began his early experiments with organic growing. In 1982, he set up an organic vegetable plot, which was pretty disastrous because, as he learnt, going organic takes time, not only in getting the soil in good heart, but also in establishing the balance between

pests and their predators. The following year, he conducted trials using chemical and non-chemical methods of pest control on cabbages and found that the foam squares sitting snugly around each plant were as effective as chemicals in keeping cabbage root fly away.

The trial ground was also the site of one of Geoff's most popular ventures, the £2-a-week garden (see page 88).

By 1983, with Barnsdale now the programme's main base, Geoff was running out of room. Late that year, Geoff heard about a property a mile away – a Victorian farmhouse called The Grange, with five acres of land. The upshot was that he bought it and set about transforming a field into an outdoor television studio. The new garden was also named 'Barnsdale'.

There was woodland to the front and the side of the house and a walled garden immediately behind it which had been used as a vegetable plot. A greenhouse was put up right away, as they needed somewhere to film if the weather was impossible. And since the site was flat and bare, with John Kenyon's approval, a dozen big mature trees were planted, which was a major undertaking involving huge lorries and cranes.

Geoff's plan was to start closest to the house by putting a gate in the walled garden and developing that area first. This was to be the centrepiece for the whole site, the pivot around which other small gardens would be developed for the programme over time. Named 'Versailles' by John Kenyon, it was a long rectangle of lawn, with deep mixed borders on either side and a beech hedge planted across the end to screen off the rest of the empty five acres. The focal point was a beautiful stone urn. It was expensive and Geoff had to choose between it and a new suit. Given Geoff's enduring and total lack of interest in clothes, it was no contest.

The first of the small gardens that became Barnsdale's trademark was the *Garden from Scratch*, done to show new gardeners how to create a garden on a virgin plot. It was reincarnated a few years later as a budget garden, and then in 1992 as *The Living Garden* for the series of the same name. The allotment area on the west side of the garden was also developed early on, since vegetables were an important element in the programme. The shed – to make it a proper allotment – wasn't added until the Dig for Victory strand in the programme in 1995 commemorating the fiftieth anniversary of VE day.

Soon after, in 1986, came the first pond and bog garden, designed primarily to attract wildlife with its shallow, sloping shore. Almost ten years later, in 1995, Geoff created a meandering stream that emptied into another pond and a bog garden, designed to be easy to construct, and to fit into an average-sized garden (see page 92).

The mid 1980s saw the creation of the rose garden. While over fifty different varieties took centre stage, this was not designed in the old style with nothing but roses planted in bare soil. Here they were underplanted with perennials and ground cover, and with other climbers, to create a garden that looked just as good when the roses were past their peak.

Although the allotment area was dedicated to fruit and veg, Geoff realised that many gardeners don't have allotments, or room in their own gardens, for a large, dedicated vegetable plot. In 1986, he laid out the Elizabethan vegetable garden. This not only looked good, with the beds edged with olive-green stained timber and red finials at the corners, but demonstrated the benefits of the deep-bed system for producing maximum yields from a small area. Crops were closely planted and all the work was done from the side paths. The deep boxes at the back were filled with gritty compost enabling asparagus, which would have struggled in Barnsdale's heavy clay soil, to thrive.

The year 1996 saw the building of the parterre garden. The size of a small back garden, 15 x 9m (50 x 30ft), this was designed to show that you could have an attractive garden that was a delight to be in, but which just happened to be mainly productive. There were formal beds for vegetables, trained fruit trees, with ornamental plants growing up obelisks placed in some of the beds, and honeysuckle over the arbour.

Geoff also undertook many smaller-scale projects, sometimes with visiting experts, like the border for winter colour planted up with Adrian Bloom in 1988. There were the famous artificial rocks (see page 90), scented borders, and the island bed for garden thugs. The idea was that certain plants had such bad reputations for invasiveness that most gardeners avoided them. Geoff wanted to see, first of all, whether they could be contained and, if so, which was the biggest thug of all. He planted *Campanula poscharskyana*, *Campanula takesimana*, *Sinacalia tangutica*, *Houttuynia cordata* 'Chameleon' and *Linaria dalmatica*. The bed was surrounded by lawn so that any escaping shoots are regularly cut off by the mower. So far, nothing has ever escaped and *Sinacalia* is the biggest thug of all.

The last garden Geoff created, in 1996, was the reclaimed garden, which featured only recycled materials. He had just installed the water feature, an old copper water tank, carefully crafted to look like a rose, when he died.

Unlike all the other gardens that have been the home of *Gardeners' World*, Barnsdale, run by Geoff's son Nick very much according to his dad's philosophy, is open to the public.

Clay Jones

Presenter 1980 – 1985

Born in 1923 in Welsh-speaking west Wales, and christened David Clay-Jones to keep his mother's maiden name (Clay) alive, he grew up on a small farm without electricity or running water just outside Cardigan. Clay's first experience of gardening was growing vegetables for the family, which started a fascination with seeds that lasted all his life.

He was a bright boy. He passed the 11+ and had applied to the University of Wales, Aberystwyth, when the war intervened and he was called up in 1942. He became a second lieutenant with the 2nd battalion, the Welsh Regiment, winding up as a captain in the 1945 Burma campaign. On his return to the UK in 1946, he read botany, zoology and chemistry at Aberystwyth. After graduation, he worked briefly as a gardener then took a job with Bees Seeds in Liverpool. Five years later he moved to Cuthberts of Llangollen as production manager. As it expanded, Clay's role expanded too and he eventually became marketing director of the whole group.

Clay had a rich baritone voice (at 17 he was invited to join the D'Oyly Carte opera company), so he was natural for radio. In the early 1960s, he made his debut, in Welsh, on *Garddio*. He broadcast in English, too – as a guest on *In Your Garden* and, in 1962, was invited to appear on *Gardening Club*. Clay once fell foul of its famous glassless greenhouse when he passed Percy a tray of seedlings straight through it.

When *Gardening Club* gave way to *Gardeners' World*, Clay was a frequent guest and, in 1980, became a regular presenter, appearing mainly at Barnsdale, though what he most enjoyed was travelling the country and meeting gardeners. Radio remained his great love. He did *Garddio* for 29 years, never missing a broadcast and, in 1976, Ken Ford, producer and chairman of *Gardeners' Question Time*, invited him to become a panellist. In 1984, Ken Ford died, and Clay took over as chairman, a job he held with great pride until ill-health forced him to retire in 1993.

By the mid 1980s, Clay found the pressure of regular television and radio appearances too much so he gave up *Gardeners' World*, concentrating on radio. Although Clay had spent much of his working life in horticulture through a time of rapid change, he gardened as he had as a boy, using only manure or compost to feed the soil, using no chemicals, and he shared Geoff Hamilton's opposition to the use of peat. Once good alternatives came along, he felt anyone still using peat ought to be 'buried in a runner-bean trench and heavily mulched with pig manure'. In 1990, he was awarded an OBE for services to gardening and broadcasting in Wales, a source of great pride on all three counts.

Clay Jones died in July 1996 aged seventy-three following a heart operation.

Geoffrey Smith

Presenter 1980 – 1982

Born in 1928, son of a head gardener, Geoffrey Smith wanted to become a forester and so went to work for the Forestry Commission. Though he loved trees, he disliked being a civil servant, and soon left to work under this father at Barningham Park, in North Yorkshire. With a fifty-acre woodland garden full of rhododendrons, he knew that he had found his niche.

After studying horticulture at Askham Bryan College, he took a job managing a commercial holding producing lettuces and bedding plants but soon became bored and left to join an experimental research station in Cornwall. He enjoyed the work but found the bureaucracy intolerable and so, at the age of twenty-six, returned to Yorkshire, to the new garden of Harlow Carr in Harrogate, as a journeyman gardener. Within three weeks he had been promoted to foreman, within three months to head gardener and, not long after, he became superintendent, a post he held for nearly twenty years.

His television career began in dramatic fashion. Paul Morby, producer of *Gardening Club*, had come to Harlow Carr to interview committee members as potential guests. Geoffrey meanwhile, who had been high-pruning an oak tree, came sliding down a rope and startled Morby half to death. After a restorative cup of tea, he invited Geoffrey to appear. For his first appearance, he talked solo about Michaelmas daisies for twelve minutes, live. He became

a frequent contributor both to *Gardening Club* and later to *Gardeners' World*. More broadcasting work followed. He joined the *Gardeners' Question Time* panel and embarked on a number of his own television series: *Mr Smith's Vegetable Garden*, *Mr Smith's Flower Garden* and so on.

After Peter Seabrook left *Gardeners' World* in 1979, Geoffrey became a main presenter with Clay Jones, appearing mainly with Arthur Billitt at Clack's Farm but also at Barnsdale as well. By the end of 1982, though, about to start work on *Geoffrey Smith's World of Flowers*, which would take him all over the globe and, with *Gardeners' Question Time* and *Gardeners' Direct Line* also taking up his time, he decided to leave *Gardeners' World*.

Since then he has made other television series – on walking rather than gardening, written many articles and books, and carried on appearing on radio. He still contributes to his local station, BBC Radio North Yorkshire, but spends as little time as possible away from his garden and the Yorkshire countryside that he loves.

He enjoyed television but found the resulting fame a double-edged sword. He recalls standing at a urinal once when he was tapped on the shoulder by a man who wanted to know why white lines were appearing on the leaves of his chrysanthemums … First and foremost, Geoffrey insists, he was and is a gardener.

Barleywood

When Alan Titchmarsh took over as the main presenter of *Gardeners' World* in August 1996, he had been developing his garden near Alton in Hampshire for fourteen years, so it was already well established. It wasn't called 'Barleywood' then. That was a name Alan came up with literally minutes before the *Radio Times* went to press with the billing for the first programme to come from there. In 1999, it became the name of a range of garden products and, from then on, given the BBC's rules about commercial exploitation, Alan had to refer to it on air as 'my Hampshire garden' instead.

It was a very challenging site – a steep slope of one in four rising from the back of the house with soil that is heavy clay with a liberal sprinkling of chalk and flint and, compared to The Magnolias, Clack's Farm or the second Barnsdale, rather small. It was one and a third acres but an acre of that was paddock near the top, so only one-third of an acre was actual garden.

Faced with the prospect of doing thirty-six programmes a year with about four items a programme, Alan quickly realised that his existing patch was much too small and so he would have to develop the paddock too. Although he took over at very short notice on the sudden death of Geoff Hamilton in August 1996, he had already started work on some new areas of the garden ready for the planned handover the following Easter.

The pond, which measures about 6 x10m (20 x 30ft), was the first major project. At first, given the chalky nature of the soil, the hole looked huge and white and gave Alan a few anxious moments, but once the liner was in, filled with water, and planted, he knew he had been right to be bold.

While obviously the garden was very much Alan's own domain, as the programme's base it also had to reflect the world of gardening and the changes in it. One of the major trends during the late 1980s and 1990s resulted from the

change in climate, which meant that plants which previously hadn't been hardy in our gardens could now survive all but the toughest of winters. So Mediterranean plants became increasingly popular and, in 1997, Alan's major project was the Mediterranean garden.

He had had a large and stylish greenhouse built on a flat area towards the top of the garden, which was beautiful as well as functional and formed the ideal backdrop for a formal Mediterranean garden. It had eight cross-shaped beds, surrounded by more beds, a small circular pool with a simple fountain in the centre and, as focal points, pencil-thin cypresses (*Cupressus sempervirens* 'Stricta') in the centre of each cross.

The planting in the beds was Mediterranean in feel. Lavender, with golden-yellow *Bidens* running through it, and deep magenta *Lychnis coronaria* 'Gardeners' World' with woolly grey leaves, combined perfectly with *Cerinthe major* 'Purpurascens'. There were orange, lemon and olive trees in pots and tubs, which spent the summers outside, but were taken into the greenhouse before the first frosts in the autumn.

But it wasn't just a question of reflecting trends. It was also a question of setting them although, as Alan says, it was not something at the forefront of his mind when he tackled something new. Indeed, had he thought that his whims and fancies would suddenly be described as 'major new trends' by the press, perhaps he wouldn't have done anything at all…

In 1997, for example, Alan turned a rather dreary area close to the house, where they used to keep chickens, into an attractive sitting area by laying decking and putting up a trellis screen, which he stained a rich blue. The sales of decking began to soar (this was before *Ground Force* began and boosted sales still further) and 'Barleywood Blue' went on to become the top-selling colour for fences and trellis. Alan feared that his obituary would read 'The Man Who Planked Britain'.

His deck lasted until 2001, when it was taken up and replaced with imitation pale terracotta tiles as part of a facelift he gave the whole area, turning it into a small courtyard potager. It's right by the back door and much handier for the odd lettuce or handful of herbs than trekking up the hill to the vegetable plot. The trellis that started it all changed colour when the deck went and became a subtle grey-green to match the conservatory.

Every year, Alan did several new projects for the programme, some large, some small. In 1998, for example, there was the seaside garden (see pages 96–97). In 1999, the tropical garden was born, pushing the bounds of hardiness beyond the Mediterranean and very much inspired by what Christopher Lloyd had done at Great Dixter, replacing the roses with bananas, cannas and ginger lilies and so on.

Alan's tropical garden is certainly a blaze of colour in late summer and early autumn with the hot colours coming not only from gazanias, New Guinea hybrid *Impatiens*, and fiery crocosmias, but from the foliage of some cannas and coleus, the flame nettle, too.

In contrast, and acknowledging the fact that many gardeners have to cope with shade, Alan developed the area under the group of large oaks, which cast dense shade from April until late autumn. The aim was to make a woodland garden with plants that can cope not only with dense shade but with poor, dry, starved, root-filled soil. Given the challenging nature of Barleywood soil at the best of times, this involved laborious cultivation followed by a thick layer of well-rotted horse manure. Alan built a hexagonal deck with gazebo above it, and placed two decking squares painted silvery grey to break up the bark paths that meandered through the shade-tolerant planting – Japanese maples and viburnums, as well as hostas, ferns, primulas, hardy geraniums and dicentras.

Sometimes, of course, Alan just indulged himself. He is passionate about tree ferns but, sensitive to the fact that they are very expensive, he limited himself to just one initially. But then he wanted more, so he snuck them in a few a time until there were seventeen of them in the end, ranging in height from 15cms (6in) to 2.4m (8ft). Alan's justification for this indulgence was that the viewers could share them with him.

In 2000, Alan, foolishly he now says, decided to enter the National Begonia Society's championships even though it broke one of his Gardening Presenter's Rules – never, ever enter any competition because, as sure as eggs is eggs, you are going to fall flat on your face. And so it proved. Having started off a dozen or so tubers, he had produced some pretty good plants. What was needed, though, were plants with either three or four stems for the multi-stem classes, or a single stem for those classes. Many of Alan's begonias had two stems. He had pinned his remaining hopes on 'Party Dress', in his own words, a variety of unsurpassed vulgarity. Then, just before the show, while the flowers looked fine from the front, the petals at the back were already beginning to die off. They had peaked too early.

But 2000 had its triumphs too, such as Alan's modern alpine beds (see page 98), a far more appropriate setting in urban gardens for these jewel-like plants than a rockery.

The butterfly meadow was another project that year and it was a great success. He had created a butterfly border in 1997, using cultivated plants like *Buddleja* and sedums but, having acquired some farmland at the top of the slope a few years earlier, he had the space to think big. So Alan planted a wildflower meadow, with species that used to thrive in cornfields, such as corn cockle, corn marigolds, cornflowers and, of course, those brilliant scarlet poppies. Alan's philosophy in *Gardeners' World* was that not everyone has got room for, say, a butterfly meadow, so he'd create one at Barleywood, and everyone could share it.

In 2001, the programme's format changed with other presenters joining Alan at Barleywood every week and undertaking projects of their own – Rachel's cutting garden, for instance, inspired by Sarah Raven, or Joe's revamp of what had been Alan's blue borders.

As any really keen gardener can imagine, that gave rise to very mixed feelings. Alan liked Rachel, Joe and Chris, but

they were digging in his flowerbeds, and that was very hard. He'd find himself keeping a very close eye and made no secret of his displeasure if jobs weren't finished or if the area wasn't left tidy.

At the beginning of 2002, Alan decided it was time to move on. He had exciting new projects that would keep him busy and, after twenty-three years, he and the family were leaving Barleywood and moving to a new home a few miles away.

He was extremely sad to leave Barleywood behind but he took very little with him because, as he said, he made a garden and that's what he wanted to leave behind. Besides it's not his garden any more – Alan's garden is the new one that he's developing for himself, his family and his friends, but well away from the cameras this time.

Berryfields

For the first time since the unsuccessful experiment with allotments in Birmingham during the very early days of *Gardeners' World*, the programme's new base is not the main presenter's own garden. Instead the BBC has leased a private garden somewhere in the West Midlands, the precise location being kept deliberately vague to deter over-enthusiastic fans.

It has been given the somewhat Ambridgean name of 'Berryfields' for the purposes of the programme. The owners still live in the house, but decisions about and care of the garden has been handed over entirely to the *Gardeners' World* team – Monty Don, Chris Beardshaw and Rachel de Thame, along with the programme's three horticultural researchers and a full-time gardener.

It's an established two-acre garden with an open aspect to the south. The soil seems to be average – not too heavy, not too light – and, unusually, covers the whole range from acid to alkaline, which means that almost anything will grow in at least one part of the garden. There are already areas of mature planting, particularly around the house, such as some old shrubberies and two long herbaceous borders in an area now called the Long Garden. Although when the team first took over the garden at the beginning of 2003, these borders looked pretty unimpressive, they decided to leave well alone and see what came up. By March, they were rewarded with masses of narcissi, and early signs of plenty of herbaceous plants beginning to push through, showing the benefits of not rushing in too quickly to dig a garden over when you take it on in winter.

Adjacent to the house is a sheltered courtyard garden, mainly paved but with a small lawn, surrounded on three side by walls and buildings, but open to the south, with a view through the Long Garden to the countryside beyond. That's where Rachel de Thame will concentrate initially: 'It 's like the type of city garden that's so familiar to me.' Another enclosed cobbled area to the side of the house, about the size of a very small city garden, is also the perfect location for container gardening, with the

emphasis on plants that like sheltered conditions. There's an existing formal pool in need of some renovation and a couple of old apple trees that they plan to make the foundation for a new orchard.

The majority of the garden, however, is grass. That means it's virtually a blank canvas giving the team ample opportunity to make their mark. What makes the new series different is that the garden won't be one person's vision or passion – it will be that of three people, all with very different, but equally significant, ideas about what a garden should be. They are all adamant that this will not be yet another TV makeover, albeit on an epic scale. 'The changes will be no less dramatic for taking place over the long term,' Monty said, 'and will make sense to viewers used to tackling their own gardens over years, not weeks.'

Although Chris Beardshaw is perhaps best known in his television work as a plantsman, he is also a trained garden designer and he is excited by the possibilities Berryfields offers to combine the two. It is, he says, a great opportunity to show that good gardening and good design go hand in hand. You can't have one without the other, otherwise it's just a collection of plants. For Chris, the large expanse of grass immediately suggests the potential for a large pond and wildlife garden.

Monty's passion for growing vegetables meant that creating a vegetable garden was a high priority. This will be very much his domain, along with the new specially built greenhouse and cold frames within its new beech-hedge boundary, as well as a propagating house (a smaller octagonal greenhouse for raising seeds and cuttings), which has been built near the stable block, now converted into a potting shed.

In the very first programme from Berryfields, Monty planted a yew hedge, making the point that yew is much quicker than its reputation would lead you to believe and that this would be a splendid boundary in about five years' time.

In the ephemeral world of television, it's reassuring to know that *Gardeners' World* will make it to forty and beyond.

Presenter 1969 – 1976

Geoff Hamilton

Geoff was born in the East End of London in August 1936, just minutes ahead of his identical twin brother Tony. Their father Cyril earned his living as a salesman, but he was also a keen gardener, a passion that Geoff shared with him from a very early age.

He knew even then that the only thing he wanted to be when he grew up was a gardener. The family moved out to leafy Broxbourne, Hertfordshire, in 1938. As soon as they were old enough, Cyril gave the twins their own patch of garden and encouraged them to use it by growing crops like radishes and lettuces, which he then bought from them, leaving them free then to spend the money on seeds and grow whatever they liked.

Broxbourne was rural then and at the end of the road was a nursery run by Dutchman Cornelius van

Hage, who went on to found the multi-million-pound van Hage Garden Centre in Great Amwell. Geoff used to boost his pocket money working there on Saturdays and in the school holidays, and he learned a lot there about plants and gardeners. Like all other eighteen year olds in the early 1950s, Geoff had to do two years' National Service. He and Tony enlisted in the RAF, were posted to the same squadron and spent much of their two years in Germany, where Geoff found time to grow tomatoes on the station's pig farm which Tony ran.

Back in civvie street, he spent two years at Writtle College taking a diploma in horticulture, then started his working life in commercial horticulture, first in a nursery, growing tomatoes, then in one growing a wider range of ornamental plants.

In the early 1960s, Geoff set up his own business, a landscaping company designing and building gardens. He loved the work – it combined all the elements he liked best about gardening – but he was not a good businessman. He disliked dealing with money, was embarrassed about asking for what the job was worth, or for what he was owed, and paperwork was very low down on his list of priorities.

In the winter of 1963, when there was snow on the ground from New Year to Easter, it was impossible to get a spade into the soil, but Geoff felt obliged to go on paying his workforce even though there was nothing to do and, worse, no money coming in. The result was that the business went bust.

His second attempt at running his own business a few years later – the Hamilton Garden Centre just outside Kettering – was no more successful. Geoff wanted to grow the plants that excited him and to share that enthusiasm with his customers. He was happy to spend hours talking plants with people, giving them advice and sometimes even visiting their gardens, whether they bought anything or not. Unfortunately, many customers only wanted to buy the plants that Geoff considered boring and therefore didn't grow. In 1973, the garden centre went bust as well.

By then, however, Geoff had been writing regularly on a freelance basis for the weekly *Garden News* and after the garden centre folded, it was in journalism that he found his niche. He was offered a staff job as a writer on *Garden News* and, not long after, he became editor of a monthly magazine in the same stable, *Practical Gardening*. The magazine was in need of a facelift and Geoff decided to make it exactly what it said on the cover – practical gardening. 'Cheap and cheerful' became Geoff's mantra and his delight in knocking things up for 'a couple of bob' was evident even then.

He had had a brief taste of television in the early 1970s while he was still running the garden centre. On the recommendation of his editor on *Garden News*, he had auditioned for, and got a job, as one of the presenters on Anglia's new show *Gardening Diary*, but that fell victim to the early shutdown of television every night that resulted from the miners' strike in 1973–1974.

In 1979, Geoff engineered a meeting with John Kenyon, who had just become the producer of *Gardeners' World*. For the first couple of years after he joined the programme, Geoff carried on as editor of *Practical Gardening* but then, with so many demands on his time, he decided to resign his job and go freelance.

As well as hosting *Gardeners' World* for seventeen years, Geoff wrote for many magazines and newspapers, including *Gardeners' World Magazine*, *Radio Times* and the *Daily Express*, and produced over twenty books. He also made a number of other television series, including *Going to Pot*, with Susan Hampshire, *First Time Garden*; *First Time Planting* and *Old Garden, New Gardener* with Gay Search, and *The Ornamental Kitchen Garden*.

Bâ Cottage Gardens, which was transmitted early in 1995, was a huge success, attracting six million viewers, as was *Paradise Gardens*, the series he had all but completed when he died suddenly of a heart attack in August on a charity bike ride for Sustrans in the Brecon Beacons. He was buried, in his boots and jeans, on what would have been his sixtieth birthday.

Geoff's impact was enormous: his down-to-earth, practical, accessible and cost-conscious approach turned so many people on to gardening. And almost single-handedly he took organic gardening out of the realm of the cranky and into the mainstream. It's probably significant that the sales of peat, which had been declining before his death, are on the increase again.

Small Gardens

Derek Jarman's Garden

'I shouldn't have become involved in cinema – that's for fools. Gardening is central in entering into another time – the elements, the returns, the cycles ... these are the resurrection cycles in my life.'

So said the film maker and, latterly, gardener, Derek Jarman in 1991 when he knew he was dying from Aids. Certainly the extraordinary garden he created on the beach at Dungeness in Kent is just as significant an achievement as his films and, according to his companion, the actor Keith Collins, who still tends it, the closer he was to death the more important the garden became. Derek Jarman had found the beach cottage that was to become his home in 1986 and, despite the looming presence of the huge nuclear power station nearby, fell in love with the place. In the book he wrote about the garden, he described the landscape as having 'the face of an angel with a naughty smile'.

Initially, the idea of creating a garden on pure shingle with no soil seemed crazy. But one day he scraped out a hole, planted a dog rose, *Rosa canina*, and staked it with a curious piece of driftwood that he found and one of the curious necklaces made of stones that he used to hang on the walls. 'The garden,' he said, 'had begun.'

At first people thought he was creating a garden for magical purposes, that he was a white witch out to 'get' the nuclear power station nearby, an idea encouraged by the curious sculptures of flotsam and stones arranged in patterns. 'It did have magic ,' Derek said, 'the magic of surprise.' He began to scoop out holes in the shingle –

no simple task because as you scoop so shingle runs back in – and filled them with manure in which to plant. The plants were then, as he put it, plonked in and left to take their chances with the Dungeness wind and the salt spray.

He grew indigenous plants like sea kale, *Crambe maritima*, which is a feature of the beach there anyway, thrift, *Armeria maritima*, and the yellow horned-poppy, *Glaucium flavum*. He also introduced non-natives that thrived in seaside conditions, like the Californian poppy, *Eschscholzia californica*, which seeds itself around so happily it is almost a weed and, surprisingly, irises. Keith Collins believes that, in summer, the irises may enjoy the dry, baking heat that they do get in Kent sometimes. Silver-leaved plants, such as *Helichrysum*, lavender, and cotton lavender, *Santolina*, and spiky sea holly, *Eryngium*, also do very well in those conditions.

There are also raised beds for herbs and vegetables, made from railway sleepers, but because Dungeness is a Site of Special Scientific Interest, you are not allowed to import soil, so Derek made his own by composting straw and plant matter from the garden.

The garden survives as a living memorial to Derek Jarman, but it is also still evolving. 'The whole garden is about evolution,' Keith says, 'and it has to change. You couldn't fix it at a certain date. What would that date be? The year before Derek died? The day he died?' Derek Jarman was in no doubt about the importance of the garden to him. 'Some gardens are paradise,' he said. 'Mine is one of them.'

Jekyll in SW19

You might think that any garden designed by Gertrude Jekyll, one of the most influential designers of the early twentieth century, must belong in the Large Gardens category. Not so.

Throughout the 1992 season of *Gardeners' World* , Liz Rigbey followed a fascinating detective story as Chris and Sue Spencer, who lived in Merton Park, near Wimbledon, set out to recreate the original Jekyll garden that surrounded their suburban Edwardian home. The story began in 1982, when the previous owner, actor Stratford Johns of *Z Cars* fame, had mentioned that what was then an ordinary suburban garden had been designed originally by a woman with a strange name. When some detective work confirmed that it was indeed Gertrude Jekyll, the Spencers decided they would find out as much as they could about the original garden and restore it. There were some early photographs showing part of the layout and the hedges, but sadly, apart from one small fragment they found in the loft, the garden plans had disappeared, so some garden archaeology was called for.

Using a pitchfork, Chris went over the lawn. Areas where he hit stones and it was hard to push the prongs in very far, he assumed had always been lawn. Where the fork went in more easily, that was where the beds had once been. When they peeled back the turf, they found, not one long bed, but two rectangular beds with one square one in the centre. Other diggings revealed the remains of flint walls, while visitors who remembered the gardens in the past added helpful information.

The son of the architect, for example, remembered George Hadfield, for whom the house was built, peering over the hedge. 'So the hedge had to be "peepable over" height,' said Chris Spencer, 'and we knew that George Hadfield was six feet tall, so that made the hedge about 5ft 8in.' They approached the Godalming Museum, which has a large collection of Gertrude Jekyll's papers, to see whether they had garden plans or planting lists, but initially were told they had nothing on Mostyn Road. But the museum thought they might like to see a list of the documents they did have on other gardens and on it, the Spencers found plant lists – in Miss Jekyll's own handwriting as it turned out – for 'Merton [Park]', their garden. Knowing what she planted was a huge help but, of course, it did not tell them where she planted it.

Penelope Hobhouse, leading garden designer, historian and biographer of Gertrude Jekyll, paid them a visit to offer some suggestions. 'I think the list is only a partial list because some of the plants that she always used, like *Alchemilla mollis* and *Caryopteris* are not there. They could certainly add these preferred plants to what is on the list.'

The most important thing, Penelope Hobhouse believed, was to plant according to Jekyllian principles: associating complementary colours and planting in drifts, not blocks. They planted the first plant – one of a hundred and fifty yews for the hedges – in November 1991 and, by August 1992, the garden was unrecognisable. The yew, allegedly slow, had put on a foot or more in height and the borders were full of colour. Hardly surprisingly, the Spencers hadn't got it all right first time.

The colours didn't flow as rhythmically into each other as they hoped, and what were meant to be drifts, which they had carefully marked out with sand on the bare soil, had somehow come out as clumps. By the mid 90s though Miss Jekyll would have been very pleased.

Jungle in the Midlands

What has made *Gardeners' World* unique over the years is that it has shown generations of gardeners how to do it properly, but it's always enjoyable to meet gardeners who, having learnt all the rules, then break them to stunning effect. Peter Bridgens' remarkable small, square garden – 12 x 12m (40 x 40ft) – in Halesowen, west of Birmingham, is a case in point. It contains a whole range of plants from *Watsonia* to *Beschorneria* , *Hedychium* to *Callistemon*, which all the gardening books tell you are not hardy in his neck of the woods. Fortunately the plants can't read and they are thriving, having come through the last few winters with just a bit of protection on the few occasions we have had a heavy frost.

When he took on this garden ten years ago, Peter inherited a raised patio across the back of the house, with a flight of concrete steps down into the main part of the garden, a hedge of leylandii, 10m (30ft) tall at the far side, and a large concrete pond in which the previous owner raised koi carp. The hedge went, while the patio and the pond – concrete 45cm (18in) thick in parts – were broken up and the materials recycled where possible.

Having read up on garden design, Peter decided that the best solution to the problems of a small square space was to design it on the diagonal, emphasising the longest axis from corner to corner. He rebuilt the patio in brick as a zig-zag, with the steps down at the centre, turning through 90 degrees at a landing halfway down. The stone and attractive pink-granite setts from the wall of the old patio were used to make the new patio and the paved central area of the garden, which he felt was too small for grass. Originally the beds were at the same level as the lower paved area, but then he decided to raise them in two tiers. 'That way I got more height at the back of the borders, and created the feeling I was after of being completely enclosed by plants.'

Originally he planted lots of herbaceous plants for instant colour, but that left the garden looking dull in the winter – a pity as it's overlooked by the patio doors and the kitchen window. So he became interested in evergreens, dramatic evergreens in particular, such as hardy palms, yuccas, phormiums and cordylines They are not reliably hardy, but do well in his garden, perhaps because he dug plenty of grit into the soil before planting. It's the combination of cold and wet that kills tender plants, and very free-draining soil gives them a better chance of survival.

That encouraged Peter to experiment further with plants that are supposedly tender, and on the patio, against the south-facing house walls, are a twining climber *Lapageria*, *Beschorneria*, a yucca-like plant from Mexico, and a coral tree, *Erythrina crista-galli*. On the patio, in a large pot is another yucca-like plant, *Dasylirion acrotrichum*, with beautiful slender spines. That isn't hardy so it spends the winter behind the sofa in the living room.

'I think people should be more adventurous and try plants that the books say they can't grow. After all, you only pay £3 or £4 for a plant – the same as you'd pay for a bunch of flowers – so even if it doesn't survive the winter, you've still had a season's pleasure from it. I must say I don't really mind losing the odd plant sometimes because it's an opportunity to grow something else.' To add to the 'hot' feel, Peter also uses plants that look exotic, but which are perfectly hardy – hostas, evergreen ceanothus trained as small trees, eucalyptus and brilliant scarlet *Crocosmia* 'Lucifer'.

He also as a very good eye for artifacts to enhance the jungly, tea-plantation feel of the garden. The lovely Chinese turquoise-glazed pots were bought at a local cash and carry, as was the hardwood steamer chair, so while they look expensive, they were not. The water feature in the corner consists of a very plain wall made from concrete blocks, with a terracotta pig's-head mask spouting water onto a trough of pebbles below, adding the cooling sound of water to a tropical garden.

Little Gem

One of the smallest proper gardens – as opposed to roof gardens, balconies, basements and so on – that *Gardeners' World* ever visited was in Gypsy Hill, south London, and belonged to Ronald Moonlight Stuart and Belinda Barnes.

It was a mere 9 x 6m (30 x 20ft) but it managed to include two areas very different in mood on different levels, and was superbly planted with interesting plants, ranging from a large acacia, *Fremontodendron*, magnolia, roses, such as 'Mermaid' and the rampageous 'Kiftsgate' and wisteria, to a fan-trained peach, with at least twenty good-sized fruits on it, and a grape vine dripping with bunches of ripening grapes. And all this in only its second season.

Remarkably, it was the first garden either of them had created. Most of the materials were salvaged from skips, with permission of course, or bought second-hand, and they did practically all the work themselves. Belinda built the 2m (6ft) high garden wall, complete with decorative bits, with Ronald mixing up the mortar, cleaning up and doing the pointing. To make the striking S-shaped wall that divides up the garden, Ronald cut hundreds of bricks, to the wedge shape required, by hand.

Most stunning gardens are the work of one person, or two people who take responsibility for different elements, but theirs is entirely a joint effort.

When they decided to design the garden, they sat down in opposite corners of the room and each drew their ideal garden. Half an hour later, when they compared them, it was as if one had been traced off the other. The pergola was in the same place, there was a lower level in each and a round water feature.

Digging out the garden, which involved demolishing an outside loo, breaking up 25cm (10in) of concrete, excavating the far end of the garden to create the difference in levels, and removing, among other things, a dead dog buried in a dustbin liner, and then building the basic structure, took about nine months of working most weekends.

It was planted in the spring of 1996 and the plants had made a phenomenal amount of growth by the following year. The acacia, for instance, was about 2.5m (8ft) tall when it went in and, having been cut back twice, just over a year later was well over 6m (19ft). Two plants of the normally slow-growing Californian jasmine,

Trachelospermum jasminoides, had completely covered the arch in the lower garden completely. The secret? Good quality top soil rescued from skips, sieved and then mixed with about a ton of well-rotted manure donated by a relative who kept ponies.

They had to rethink the rose 'Kiftsgate' quickly. While it formed a useful prickly barrier along the top of the wall, they hadn't realised how vigorous it was. It can grow up to a staggering 25m (83ft), and so the four they had planted the previous year had already been thinned to two and it was likely that one of those would soon go.

The garden was a delightful mixture of native plants, such as the exploding caper spurge, *Euphorbia lathyrus*, and sweet woodruff, *Galium odoratum*, with the more unusual, such as the wiry-stemmed, creeping foliage plant *Muehlenbeckia*, which clothed one wall. They grow lots of plants in pots, a collection of hostas, for instance, and some tender specimens, like agapanthus, which are over-wintered in Belinda's mother's greenhouse in Berkshire.

They had a watering system on a timer for the beds, but Ronald watered the pots by hand. If they went away for the weekend, he moved all the pots into the side passage, then put on his waterproofs, set the sprinkler system going, and moved the pots around to make sure they were all covered – a novel way of watering that had not been seen on *Gardeners' World* before.

Presenter 1982 – 1990

Roy Lancaster

Surprisingly perhaps, plants were not Roy's first great passion in life. His first ambition was to be a steam-engine driver and his second was to work on a nature reserve. His interest in wildlife led to an interest in wild flowers and, at 15, he helped compile a flora of his home town, Bolton in Lancashire. When he left school the same year, at the suggestion of the man at the local museum who had supervised the flora, he joined the local parks department. In his first job at Mossbank Gardens, he worked on the large rock garden there under two men who took him under their wing and started to teach him about plants. They suggested he went in half an hour early every morning, and they taught him three plants a day.

Roy did most of his National Service in Malaya, where he used his spare time collecting and pressing plants to send to the local botanical gardens and also back to Kew. His interest in tropical plants took him to the University of Cambridge Botanical Gardens as a student gardener and from there to Hillier's Nurseries in Hampshire. In 1972, he became curator of the Sir Harold Hillier arboretum, which contains one of the largest collections of hardy trees and shrubs in the temperate regions.

Since 1980, he has been freelance, plant hunting all round the world, writing many books, and broadcasting. Apart from eight years on *Gardeners' World*, there were series for Granada on the great plant collections and plant hunters and Channel 4's *Garden Club* . He is now a regular on Radio 4's *Gardeners' Question Time* and travels as much as he wants to, lecturing and judging, not only in this country but abroad. Apart from the major RHS shows here, he has judged at the Journées des Plantes at Courson for fifteen years and, most recently, at the new San Francisco Flower Show, which all takes place indoors.

The highlight of his time on *Gardeners' World* was a visit he made with Geoff Hamilton to Carnforth in Lancashire, Roy's home territory. After filming was over, Roy took Geoff up to nearby Hutton Roof and showed him the limestone pavement there, a habitat for a unique range of plants that was under threat from the increasing demand by gardeners for rockery stone. Geoff spend an hour and half exploring, and was hooked. From that day, his campaign to save the remaining limestone pavements grew.

Presenter 1983 – 1988

John Kelly

John was born in New Zealand and came to England when he was seven. Having gone to medical school, he realised that he didn't want to be a doctor like his father and, while he was marking time as a drug company rep, he developed a passion for alpine plants. Having taught himself about this fascinating group of plants, he not only won the Alpine Society's coveted Farrer Gold medal, but set up his own alpine nursery in Leicestershire in 1967.

Eleven years later he applied for, and got, the job as curator of the famous Abbotsbury Subtropical Gardens in Weymouth, Dorset. While he was there, among other things, he oversaw the creation of a rose garden, developed a plant sales area and increased the numbers of visitors. When *Gardeners' World* recorded a programme there in 1983, producer John Kenyon was impressed with both his knowledge as a plantsman and his ability to communicate, so invited him to become a regular member of the team.

In 1989, he left Abbotsbury to become a full-time writer and broadcaster, and moved to near Bantry, in the south-west of Ireland, where his wife Nicky raised horses and sheep and John tried to learn Irish. He had never gardened in their former home at Abbotsbury – a bit of a busman's holiday presumably – but here he started a collection of unusual tender plants, since the question of where the line between tender and hardy fell had long fascinated him.

He died suddenly of a brain haemorrhage at the end 1996, just a few months after Geoff Hamilton and, ironically, also just before his sixtieth birthday.

Presenter 1985 – 1986

Margaret Waddy

Although Margaret Waddy had loved plants since she spent a year at the age of four in Ghana, her route into horticulture was circuitous – from teacher to medical laboratory technician to a course in horticulture. She wound up at the now defunct National Seed Development Organisation (NSDO) in Cambridge, working on micro-propagation.

Recommended by a colleague who had appeared on *Gardeners' World*, Margaret did an interview with Clay Jones at Barnsdale and afterwards was asked to do an audition piece to camera . Despite being told that she was 'sounding more pedantic by the minute', she was invited back to present an item on how to tell good plants from bad when buying.

Margaret thoroughly enjoyed what she calls the 'ad hoc-ness' of it all – being asked to prepare an item, arrive with all the necessary stuff only to be told that she was doing something completely different. She enjoyed the company too and had a particular affection for John Kelly, who was very kind and supportive early on. He was particularly kind because, as he told her later, he was convinced she had been brought in to replace him.

Margaret kept her job at the NSDO throughout her time with the programme, stayed on through privatisation, but took early retirement in 1998. Since then, she has been the press and publicity officer for the Institute of Horticulture, which aims to promote careers in horticulture.

Presenter 1984 and 1990 – 1992

Dr Stefan Buczacki

The only television gardener always to appear in a bow tie, Stefan did a degree in botany at Southampton University, followed by a D. Phil. – hence 'Dr' Buczacki. He started his career as a plant pathologist with the National Vegetable Research Station in Warwickshire, as well as doing some lecturing at the University of Warwick. In 1981, as the result of a book he had written on mushrooms and fungi – more a hobby than a professional speciality – he was interviewed on local radio.

At the suggestion of a friend who heard it, he sent the tape to the producer of Gardeners' Question Time. His timing could not have been more perfect because the panel's resident scientist, Professor Alan Gemmell, had told the producer that week that he wanted to retire. Stefan was invited to take part in three programmes initially, which led to another six hundred over the next fifteen years. He took over the chair briefly after the sudden death of Clay Jones in 1996, before leaving the BBC with several other team members to start *Gardening Forum*, on Classic FM.

Stefan is unique in that he has two spells as a presenter on *Gardeners' World*. The first, in 1984, came as a result of

working with Clay Jones on *Gardeners' Question Time* and the second, in the early '90s, when he was brought in by the show's first female producer, Stephanie Silk.

In the meantime, he had appeared on *Good Morning with Anne and Nick* and on *Gardeners' Direct Line*, and afterwards went on to make other television appearances in *Stefan Buczacki's Gardening Road Show*, and *Stefan Buczacki's Gardening Britain*, both for BBC 2. He appeared regularly for many years on Gloria Hunniford's Channel 5 daytime show, *Open House*. He has written more than forty books over the years, the most recent being *Best Water Gardens*.

Although he has designed gardens for friends and acquaintances on an *ad hoc* basis for many years, he has recently started a garden design practice in association with a firm of architects, specialising in the restoration of period properties and in designing new houses and gardens from scratch.

Gardeners' World
Projects

£2-a-week Garden

At the beginning of 1983, Geoff Hamilton set himself a challenge. Could he maintain and improve a small garden roughly 10 x 14m (36 x 48ft) with a lawn, borders, a patio, some fruit and vegetables and a small unheated greenhouse on just £2 a week – £104 a year?

ABOVE: A recreation of the £2-a-week garden at Barnsdale Mark 2.
FAR LEFT: the 'carrycot' cold frame in use.
LEFT: The booklet that accompanied the original series.

Geoff did not cheat. He always noted down the shop price when he harvested fruit and vegetables, but didn't add the money saved to his budget. Instead he put it aside to cover unforeseen circumstances like the old mower packing up. By the end of the year, he'd saved £140 on fruit and veg – a profit of £35. £2 in 1983 is the equivalent of £4 in 2003, so today's budget gardener would have £208 to spend. Many of Geoff's money-saving tips are still applicable today. Making your own compost costs nothing if you recycle all your household vegetable waste, grass clippings, newspapers and so on. You don't even need a compost bin. Make it in old plastic sacks with air holes punched in the sides – Geoff made thirteen sacksful during the year of his experiment.

THE FLOWER GARDEN

With no money for trees or shrubs, all the colour came from hardy annuals. One packet of the tall *Lavatera* 'Silver Cup' formed a screen between the flower garden and the vegetable plot. That would cost about £1.40 today. He filled the rest of the borders with six packets of mixed seeds. At a little over a £1 a time now they are still excellent value for money. Geoff made the seeds go a long way by sowing very thinly indeed. This meant he didn't need to do much thinning out when they germinated, but where he did, he broke the rules by using the thinnings to fill any gaps. Geoff found that if you do it when the seedlings are small – about 1.25cm (½in) high – and water well before and after, you can get away with it. A packet of sweet peas, sown direct into the soil, makes an excellent cover for a fence. As support, use nylon twine, begged from local shops, factories or farms, and it will cost you nothing. You can raise perennials and alpines from seed. Perennials can be sown direct in a seedbed in a quiet corner and transplanted later, while plastic coffee cups, with drainage holes punched in the bottom, make great free flowerpots for the latter.

Containers can be improvised from plastic drums with drainage holes drilled in the bottom, or larger holes cut in the sides to make planting pockets. Once the plants are growing well, the container disappears from view.

Geoff fashioned Japanese-style hanging baskets from strips of wood recycled from packing cases, drilled at the

ABOVE: The polythene, bamboo and alkathene piping cloche in action.

corners and held together with nylon string threaded through. They were lined with thick polythene, filled with home-mixed potting compost and planted with trailing begonias, which he swapped with a friend for Brussels sprout plants. Alternatively, invest another £1 in a packet of nasturtium seeds and sow those direct.

THE VEGETABLE GARDEN

Several long-serving Barnsdale favourites came into their own here – such as the cloche made from pairs of bamboo canes pushed into the soil at intervals on each side of the bed and into lengths of alkathene piping, which formed the supporting hoops. Thin polythene – in Geoff's case, from the dry cleaning – was then stretched over them and tied to two wooden pegs at either end. There was the prototype of the carrycot cold frame – made from an orange box covered with a sheet of rigid plastic and shaded with onion sacks. Then there was the windowsill propagator also made from an orange box with the front cut out, and lined with kitchen foil to reflect light all round the seedlings and keep them stocky rather than spindly.

For seed trays, Geoff improvised with polystyrene trays in which supermarkets sell meat or fish, and foil containers from the Chinese takeaway – the trouble with pricking out a tray of seedlings, Geoff said, was that an hour later, you felt like pricking out another one. For block sowing, papier mâché egg trays are ideal. Once the seedlings are ready to be planted out, cut up the tray into individual cells and plant the whole thing, cell and all. The papier mâché will rot away in the ground.

Artificial Rocks

This project, which had some of his nearest and dearest convinced that Geoff Hamilton had finally flipped, brought together two important strands in his work – his concern for the environment and his delight in 'knocking things up' cheaply and easily. At the time, Geoff was actively involved in the campaign to stop the destruction of the limestone pavements – those unique habitats for plants, which were being rapidly depleted to provide the limestone for garden rockeries.

Make your rocks in batches. First, dig several holes in the ground, the size and roughly the shape you want your finished rocks to be. Then line each hole roughly with thick polythene – do not try to smooth it out too much because the creases and folds in the polythene are what will make the cracks and crevices in the surface of the rocks.

Pile the hypertufa into the lined holes and then, with a trowel, work it well up the sides, leaving the centre hollow and the sides a minimum of 5cm (2in) thick. This will make the rocks lighter to manoeuvre and, of course, less expensive. Reinforce very large or broad, shallow rocks. Half fill the mould, then lay a piece of chicken wire on the top of the hypertufa, bending the ends in if necessary, and then add the rest.

Leave them for a couple of days until the mixture has thoroughly dried out. Then lift the rocks out of the holes carefully and peel off the polythene. If they are a bit shiny on top, where they have been in contact with the polythene, rough them up a little with a wire brush. They will look raw and rather unconvincing at this stage, but don't worry. Once they are in position, well grouped and partly buried in the soil, and once mosses and lichens begin to grow on them (as they will) and especially once you have planted around them, they will soon look remarkably convincing.

Hypertufa

2 parts coir
2 parts sharp sand
1 part fresh cement
(it is important that it is fresh)
Yellow cement dye

Mix all the dry ingredients together with a spade, then add water to make a fairly stiff mixture.

Pond, Stream & Bog Garden

The sight and sound of moving water in the garden is delightful and, as Geoff Hamilton's 1996 project shows, by designing a meandering route, you can pack a lot of stream into a small space. Make a rough plan on paper, then translate it onto the ground using rope or hose.

You will need

Pebbles and boulders
A submersible pump (fitted by a qualified electrician).
Hose to carry the water from the pond to the start of the stream.

A fibre underliner and/or builders' sand
A butyl or thick polythene pond liner
Size = the length plus twice the depth + 30 cm (12 in) multiplied by the width plus twice the depth + 30cm (12 in)
For a pond 3m x 1.5m x 60cm deep, the liner will be 4.5m x 3m, that is: (3m + 60cm + 60cm + 30cm) x (1.5m + 60cm + 60cm + 30cm)

The stream and pond marked out with bamboo canes and sand.

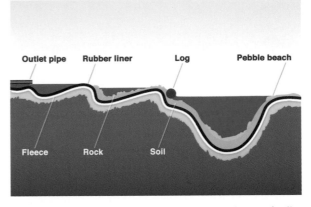

Backward-sloping stream sections retain water when the pump is off.

DIGGING OUT

Getting the levels right is vital. Water always finds its own level so if one side is higher than the other, the liner will show, spoiling the natural effect. Mark it out with pegs, each with a pencil line 5cm (2in) from the top, hammering them down until the pencil line is at soil level. Check with a spirit-level that each one is level with its neighbour. Carry on right the way round and, with luck, the last peg should be level with the first. If not, adjust the pegs until they are .

THE POND

Start with the circular pond. On very stony soil, line the hole first with a layer of builders' sand a few inches thick, and then with special polyester fibre matting to prevent stones puncturing the liner, which goes in last.

THE STREAM

For ease and economy, line the stream a section at a time, making a series of inter-linked ponds about 2m (6ft) long, between 2.4m (8ft) and 60cm (2ft) wide and about 15cm

(6in) deep. Make each slope slightly downwards away from the pond so that if the pump is switched off, all the water doesn't empty into the pond. (See diagram, above).

Fold any excess liner at the sides into neat pleats lying in the same direction as the flow. The water will then flatten them, not push them up. After trimming excess liner, leaving 15cm (6in) each side to be buried under soil, Geoff lined the stream with pebbles, for a natural look, while groups of large boulders in the middle created interesting eddies. More pebbles and boulders along the edge hid the liner. Geoff placed a submersible pump in the pond with a length of hose to carry the water back up to the inlet at the top of the stream – by clever design, only a short distance away and disguised with boulders.

Once the pond was planted up with water lilies and the bog gardens on the banks of the stream were filled with attractive marginal plants, it looked as though it had been there for ever.

Mary Spiller

Presenter 1982 – 1983

Mary made history as the first female presenter on *Gardeners' World*. Born in Oxford, she fell into gardening by accident. During the war, she wanted to train as a Land Girl at Waterperry horticultural training college for women in Wheatley near Oxford, but her father, feeling that was too strenuous, enrolled her on a short horticulture course instead. She was hooked and horticulture became her career. She returned to Waterperry in 1961 to help out with day courses for amateurs and, in 1963, took on the ornamental garden and later the management of the whole site. In that capacity she was interviewed on *Gardeners' World* in 1982 by Geoffrey Smith and, as John Kenyon was keen to add a woman to the team of presenters, he asked her to do more. So once a month or so, she travelled up to Barnsdale, or to the garden being featured and did whatever was required – usually something to do with herbaceous plants or alpines. Although now in her late seventies, and retired from management, she still teaches two days a week at Waterperry.

Anne Mayo

Presenter 1983 – 1984

Anne was working at Kew Gardens for the International Union for the Conservation of Nature when she was suggested to the team as a presenter for the programme. After her time with *Gardeners' World*, Anne dropped right out of the public eye.

Lynda Brown

Presenter 1992 – 1993

Lynda was a cookery writer who was keen to grow as many ingredients as possible and, after *Gardeners' World* visited her garden, she was invited to establish a small cook's garden at Barnsdale. She grew vegetables primarily for flavour, and suggested ways of cooking them, which led to the famous complaint from one viewer who wanted to know 'what all this cooking nonsense has to do with growing vegetables'. Lynda shared Geoff's commitment to growing organically and since then has become widely regarded as an authority on organic food. Her most recent books are *Organic Living* and *The New Shoppers' Guide to Organic Food*.

Vanessa Collingridge

Presenter 1994 – 1995

Vanessa, who was based in Scotland, was a journalist with a background in geography, rather than a horticulturist. After *Gardeners' World*, she became a reporter for the Channel 5 current affairs programme, *What's the Story*, as well as contributing to ITV's *Tonight* with Trevor McDonald.

Most recently she wrote a biography of Captain Cook and her ancestor George Collingridge, who also went to Australia about 100 years later. Based on maps he uncovered, he insisted that the Portuguese had discovered the continent before Captain Cook, which made him extremely unpopular.

Valerie Waters

Presenter 1996 – 1998

Valerie Waters was working part-time in a Dublin garden centre and on BBC Northern Ireland's gardening show when she met Geoff Hamilton and enterprisingly handed him a VCR of her TV work. After *Gardeners' World*, she worked for RTE on *The Garden Show*, and on other programmes as a reporter. In 2001, she returned as the gardener to the Tyrone Guthrie Centre in Co. Monaghan. She now works there three days a week and, on the other two days, as a journalist covering environmental and rural affairs for RTE's *Nationwide*.

Seaside Garden

Alan Titchmarsh, being a sailor and passionate about the sea, loves the seaside, so rather than pine for it when he got back from his holidays, he turned the area behind The Far Pavilion – the summerhouse that was transformed into his writing room when he became a novelist – into a seaside garden.

Laying a cobble path

Mark the curves with hosepipe or washing line and then dig out the path to a depth of about 10–15cm (4–6in).

Line it with polythene. Working on about a metre (3ft) at a time – about as far as you can comfortably reach forward when you're kneeling – fill in with a stiff mix of six parts aggregate to one part cement. Use a float to level it out.

This mix is too dense to lay the cobbles in, so on top you need a shallower layer – about 2.5cm (1in) – of three parts sharp sand to one part cement. Float this carefully over the top and then start to lay the Caledonian cobbles, tamping them down with a rubber mallet. To cope with excess water once the path is finished, either make it with a gentle camber, so the water drains off on both sides, or with a gentle slope in one direction.

Fill in the gaps between the cobbles with smaller Caledonian pebbles. Leave it to set for about a week, then go over it with a stiff brush and the hose, to get rid of any cement remaining on the surface of the cobbles.

The look involves rather sparse, dune-like planting in among chunky cobbles, shingle and sand, along with a few nautical accessories such as the woven lobster pots. The first task was to lay a winding path of cobbles set in cement. Once the garden was completed, this would blend in with the surrounding cobbles and shingle and not look like a separate path at all, but it would always be a firm, dry surface to walk on.

Under the sand for the small 'beach', Alan laid porous weed-suppressing membrane, while on the soil around the planting, a thick layer of sharp sand beneath the shingle and the cobbles served the same purpose.

The seating area, large enough to take a deckchair, was made from black painted sleepers used as decking, with a few of different heights used upright at the back to create the feeling of breakwaters on a beach.

To screen the whole area from the rest of the garden, Alan used woven-willow panels, in front of which was a thin screen of bamboo, which rustles in the breeze to produce a sound suggesting, to those with boundless imagination, the waves sucking at a shingle shore.

Alan used plants sparingly in the garden. Some of them were natives like the hummock-forming thrift, *Armeria maritima*, while others were spiky, such as the phormiums and a variegated yucca. A clump of the magnificent coppery pheasant's tail grass, *Stipa arundinacea*, which sways in the slightest breeze, adds movement to the area.

The accessories were very important in setting the mood – woven wicker lobster pots, for example, and a stripy blue and white deckchair say 'seaside' loud and clear.

Inspired by Derek Jarman's extraordinary beach garden at Dungeness, Alan created wonderful sculptures with pebbles and lengths of metal-reinforcing rods. Some consisted of pebbles drilled part through at the bottom and perched on top of rods. Others involved drilling right through the pebbles and stacking them on the rods.

Many of these are in the extension to the seaside garden, the grass garden, which is more densely planted with bamboos and grasses – mostly annual – but which is also mulched with shingle and cobbles.

Modern Alpine Beds

Instead of a rockery at steeply sloping Barleywood, Alan decided to make a series of raised alpine beds that would be an attractive feature in any garden, sloping or flat. Alan made two groups of interlocking rectangular boxes of different heights, separated by a gravel path, but obviously you can make any combination you like.

To work out the materials you will need, make a rough sketch first. You'll need one pressure-treated 135cm (4ft 6in) planed-all-round (PAR) post for each corner, plus lengths of tanalised timber 15 x 5cm (6 x 2in) to make the sides – one, two or three lengths per side depending on the height you want – and 10cm (4in) galvanised nails to hold it all together. Start by marking out your design with a tape measure and bamboo canes. Take the time to get this exactly right, otherwise you'll have problems later on. Once

that's done, mark the outline on the soil with sand to give you a clear idea of the finished shape. If you are not happy with it, it's simple to change it at this stage.

Hammer in the posts – you'll need an extra pair of hands to hold them steady while you bang them in – and keep checking with a spirit level to make sure that they are going in straight. They need to go into the ground about 30cm (12in). Then measure and cut the wood to length – much safer to leave the cutting until the posts are in – and nail it on to the posts. A useful tip: standing with one knee pressed against the post will keep it stable while you bang the nails in on the other side.

Once it's all done, trim the posts, preferably with an inward-sloping cut, so that when the beds are filled and top-dressed, you won't see them at all. Once the wood has been stained – Alan chose a black woodstain to set off the plants – half-fill each box with rubble or crocks to ensure the good drainage that these plants enjoy.

With separate boxes, you can give each type of alpine the soil conditions it prefers. Some that like very sharp drainage can have very gritty mixture of multipurpose compost, sharp sand or fine grit and sieved leaf mould – while others, the woodlanders, such as dwarf rhododendrons and hardy cyclamen, can have an acidic, leafier mix that retains moisture better. Although you don't need rocks to grow rock plants, a few pieces of attractive rock will add texture to your trough. In the woodlanders'

trough, Alan used chunks of birch for the same purpose.

Although you may be tempted to buy everything that 's flowering at that moment when you buy your plants, restrain yourself, and ensure you choose some that flower at different times so that your alpine beds look good for the longest season.

Alan's selection included trailers, such as *Genista lydia* and *Saxifraga* 'Tumbling Waters', clump-formers, like *Campanula carpatica*, rosette-formers like houseleeks, *Sempervivum*, carpeters, such as the golden thyme, *Thymus pulegioides* 'Goldentime', and, for height, very slow-growing dwarf conifers, such as *Juniperus communis* 'Compressa'.

Once the plants are in, mulch the well-drained beds with an inch or so of gravel, and the woodlanders with chipped bark. Gravel not only looks good, it also keeps the plants' foliage off the soil and stops it rotting. The easiest way to apply it is to snip off the corner of the bag and pipe it on like icing.

Anne Swithinbank

Anne's gardening career started at the nursery of her local parks department in Bexley, Kent. She loved the work and only left because she had a place on the diploma course at the Royal Botanic Gardens, Kew. From there she went to work as nursery foreman for the parks department in Epsom, Surrey, which she thoroughly enjoyed, but realised, after a year or two that, as centralised growing was coming in, the days of local parks' nurseries were numbered. She was looking around for a new job when she heard that the Royal Horticultural Society was looking for a glasshouse supervisor in its garden at Wisley. She applied and got the job.

While she was there, Channel 4 was filming *Gardeners' Calendar*, a series that observed Wisley's team of experts at work. For Anne, it was an ideal introduction to television because she wasn't required to be a presenter as such and talk to camera. Instead she simply did what she would normally do and talked about it while the cameras rolled. As a result, she was spotted by one of the occasional directors on *Gardeners' World*, Phil Franklin, who invited her up to Barnsdale as a guest. She quickly became a regular where her domain was the greenhouse, and her speciality – indoor plants and containers. Like

Margaret Waddy, her immediate predecessor, she also became used to arriving at Barnsdale with plants and accessories that she had sometimes driven miles to pick up, only to be told that she was doing something quite different instead. Although Anne did travel to other gardens to interview the owners, she enjoyed the Barnsdale filming days most because of the cameraderie and the humour.

After *Gardeners' World*, Anne made a number of other television series – *The Real Gardening Show* for the cable channel Cable 1, two series of *Bloom* for C4, as well as *Gardens of the Caribbean*.

She became one of the regular panellists on *Gardeners' Question Time* in 1996, and still writes regularly for *Gardeners' World Magazine*, *Amateur Gardening* and the *Western Morning News*. Five years ago, she moved to Devon with her family and has developed a large garden there with the help of her husband John, who she met at Kew. He has become a garden photographer, so they now work on magazine and book projects together using the garden as an outdoor studio.

Presenter 1989 – 2002

Pippa Greenwood

The queen of bugs, slugs and other thugs, Pippa has gardened since childhood. Her first horticultural memory is of planting marigolds with her mum when she was three.

She trained as a botanist at Durham University, and followed that with an MSc in crop protection at Reading University. From there, she went on to run the Royal Horticultural Society's plant pathology department at Wisley, Surrey. During the 11 years she was there, she answered thousands of gardening queries.

She was spotted on the Royal Horticutural Society's stand at the Chelsea Flower Show in 1987 by BBC producer Mark Kershaw ,who thought her encyclopedic knowledge of plant pests and diseases as well as her bubbly personality made her a natural for television gardening programmes.

After appearing on daytime programmes, she joined *Gardeners' World* in 1989 and became the programme's second longest-serving presenter after Geoff Hamilton. Although she covered a variety of topics for *Gardeners'*

World , she was the programme's undisputed expert on pests and diseases, as well as on the science of horticulture. Although in her early days, she and Geoff Hamilton were on different sides of the organic debate, she finally came round to his way of thinking.

She has been a regular panellist on *Gardeners' Question Time* since 1994, and has presented two series of *Growing Science* for Radio 4.

Pippa writes regularly for *The Mirror*, for *Ideal Home* and *Gardeners' World Magazine*. Her many books include The Royal Horticultural Society's *Pests and Diseases* (with Andrew Halstead), *The Flower Gardener*, and *Garden Problem Solver*. She travels widely lecturing and often hosts gardening cruises and holidays.

Pippa lives in rural Hampshire with her family, and regular viewers will be familiar with her hillside garden from which she has presented many items, mainly on organic fruit and vegetable growing.

A Garden in a Season

What do you do if you've just bought your first home, want a garden to enjoy but have no money left? The answer is to beg or borrow £50 and grow a whole garden from packets of seeds.

The Annuals

Reds and oranges
California poppies (*Eschscholzia californica* 'Inferno')
Pot marigolds (*Calendula officinalis*)
Nasturtiums (*Tropaeolum majus*)
Red orach (*Atriplex hortensis* 'Cupreata')
Sunflowers (*Helianthus* 'Velvet Queen'
Chrysanthemum 'German Flag')
Ipomoea lobata

Yellows
Poached egg plant (*Limnanthes douglasii*)
Annual chrysanthemum 'Primrose Gem'

Pink, Salmon and Apricot
Clarkia 'Apple Blossom'
Godetia 'Salmon Princess'
Nasturtium (*Tropaeolum* 'Tip Top Apricot')
Pot marigold (*Calendula* 'Pacific Apricot')
Runner bean 'Painted Lady' (climber)

Blues and Mauves
Love-in-a-mist (*Nigella damascena*)
Annual lupin (*Lupinus cruickshankii* 'Sunrise')
Baby-blue-eyes (*Nemophila insignis*)
Cornflowers (*Centaurea cyanus* 'Blue Ball', 'Mauve Queen' and 'Black Ball')
Morning glory (*Ipomoea indica* 'Heavenly Blue')

FAR LEFT: Marking out the areas for different types of annuals is easily done with sand poured from an empty wine bottle.
LEFT: Regular feeding and watering will keep the display going right through summer.

The plot in King's Heath Park was roughly 7 x 6m (22 x 20ft) – the size of garden that many brand new houses have.

A path and seating area was made with gravel – a good cheap temporary solution – laid over membrane to suppress weeds, in the shape of a question mark which provided good deep planting areas in the corners and created a sense of somewhere to go – important in a very small garden.

One mistake gardeners often make in small spaces is to jumble colours all up together. So we grouped our colours, starting with the really hot, fiery shades – red, orange and golden yellow, moving through softer yellows, to blues, mauves, pink, salmon, apricot and back to soft orange.

On the fences we grew annual climbers. Some, like the red and white runner bean 'Painted Lady', were sown direct into the soil. The tender annual *Ipomoea lobata*, which has sprays of red, orange and cream flowers all at the same time, was started off in pots indoors on the windowsill. It was planted out in late May in a large blue-green pot to climb up a wooden tripod stained the same colour as the fences, to give instant height – very important in a new garden. Seed was sown direct into all our other containers and hanging baskets.

Sown in late March, most of the annuals thrived and by early July the garden was ablaze with colour. By regular feeding with liquid fertiliser and judicious deadheading, the display continued well into September. But inevitably, there were a few failures. One small patch of cream Californian poppies died for no apparent reason.

While the containers were very successful, the hanging baskets were less so. The nasturtiums in them were growing strongly but then got clobbered by blackfly, which didn't touch those in the borders at all, and the sweet peas preferred climbing to trailing.

In many cases, we didn't sow the whole packet of seeds, so you can do it even more cheaply if you share, or keep the unused seeds in a plastic box in the salad drawer of the fridge for next year. And at the end of the summer, you'll also be able to harvest masses of seed, so that you can sow the whole garden again next year for free.

Ipomoea lobata.

Eschscholzia 'Inferno'.

Centaurea cyanea 'Blue Ball'.

Helianthus 'Velvet Queen'.

Healing Garden

Plants, gardens and gardening are good for us in mind, body and spirit. Just being in a leafy, green space benefits us physically, lowering our heart rate and our blood pressure. Being surrounded by beautiful plants positively does us good because when our sense of well-being is enhanced, our immune system becomes stronger.

Gardening is good for us too, not just physically, but mentally and emotionally, too. It's a great stress-buster and offers the chance to have an unpressured nurturing relationship with living things, which is why horticultural therapy is so valuable for people with mental illness. It's also an optimistic activity. By sowing a seed you are investing in the future, and gardening gives us endless second chances.

THE HEALING GARDEN

This small typical back garden, about 10m x 5m (35ft x 16ft) on an 1980s estate, was designed by Jean Goldberry to include as many healing elements as possible.

Herbs In the small herb garden, and in other beds, are culinary and medicinal herbs, such as mint, camomile, rosemary, sage and thyme.

Aromatherapy Scent, and particularly essential oils, have a powerful effect on the brain and the nervous system. Lavender, for example, induces restful sleep as effectively as some mild sleeping tablets. Choose scents to create different moods. Herbs like basil, fennel, mint, rosemary and thyme have a stimulating effect as does citrus, so choose lemon verbena, or lemon balm to surround an area of activity. For tranquillity, go for calming, relaxing or balancing scents, such as camomile, clary sage, lavender and marjoram.

Colour In the active, social area of the garden, the main colours are red, orange and yellow, with dahlias, nasturtiums and kniphofias. Red is the most stimulating colour, increasing heart rate, respiration and blood pressure and, like orange and yellow, also stimulates the appetite, so is good for an eating area. Blue is the opposite. It is a calming colour, lowering blood pressure and slowing the heart rate. Dividing the garden is a large triangular bed, planted with blue flowers, such as *Geranium sylvaticum* 'Mayflower', *Salvia* x *superba* 'Mainacht' and *Ceratostigma willmottianum*. Since a colour's effect is enhanced by a small amount of its complementary colour – in this instance, orange – there is also *Kniphofia* 'Bees Sunset' and *Crocosmia* x *crocosmiiflora* 'George Davison'.

Quiet contemplation In the second part of the garden, the main plant colour is green, with foliage plants such as evergreen bamboo, *Phyllostachys aurea*, a tree fern, *Dicksonia antarctica*, *Mahonia* x *media* 'Winter Sun', and ferns. Green is a neutral, calming colour – hence its frequent use in hospitals – and so ideal here.

Meditation A garden is an oasis of calm in a busy stress-filled world, so a quiet area is essential. Ideally, this should involve a journey to help clear your mind, so for the longest possible journey in a small garden, the path is a spiral, using small cobbles to create tight smooth curves. It's also narrow, to make you concentrate on where you are putting your feet and forget your problems. In the centre there's just room for a single seat because you want to be alone. To reinforce a strong sense of separation, you reach the quiet area by crossing the rill that extends the whole width of the garden, using stepping stones made from triangular boxes filled with white cement, topped with large, soap-bubble marbles.

Water is an aid to contemplation, both in reflective still water and the sound and light-catching movement of running water. Most of the rill is still, but at one end is a large, dark grey fibreglass sphere, out of which water comes bubbling.

Interactive Garden

In 2001, past and future came together in the Interactive garden, in which
Rachel de Thame and Joe Swift made use of the Internet in the redesigning
of a neglected garden in Birmingham.

Taking Levels

Hold a post upright at the lowest point of the garden and attach string to it. Take the other end of the string to the highest point of the garden and either get someone to hold it on the ground, or weight it down with a heavy rock or paving slab. Adjust the string on the lower post until it is level – hold a spirit level against it to check that it is – and then mark its position on the post. Measure the distance between the post and the ground. This will tell you by how much the garden slopes – in the case of the Interactive garden it was 1.3m (4ft 4in) higher at the top than the bottom – so that you can then work out how many steps you need and how big each one needs to be.

Chocolate Box

Given the Cadbury and Bourneville associations, Rachel decided it would be fun to have a 'chocolate corner', with plants that either had the word in their name or, as in the case of *Cosmos atrosanguineus*, smelled of chocolate. In addition, there was *Heuchera* 'Chocolate Ruffles', a perennial with deep maroon frilly leaves and tall, arching sprays of small creamy white flowers in midsummer, and *Helianthemum* 'Chocolate Blotch', a sun-loving, low-growing rock rose, which has burnt orange flowers with a rich chocolate-brown blotch at the centre.

The garden, over a hundred years old, was in Bourneville Village, which was built by the Quaker chocolate maker and philanthropist, George Cadbury, to house his workers. Every home he felt should have a decent-sized garden in which to grow vegetables, fruit and flowers, and he even organised gardening classes to help the residents do so.

By 2001, it was just rough grass with a couple of old fruit trees and a Christmas tree planted by a previous tenant in 1948, but now protected by a conservation order. It cast such deep shade that Joe and Rachel sought permission to lift the crown and allow more light in. The two old apple trees were the cause of some debate. Joe wanted them out because they were not particularly attractive or productive. Rachel wanted to keep them, so it was put to the vote on the *Gardeners' World* website. A convincing 88 per cent wanted the trees to stay.

What Joe set out to do in his redesign was reinterpret the garden for the twenty-first century, so there would be fruit, vegetables and flowers, and areas for play and leisure. The garden was on a slope, but Joe felt that made it more interesting than a garden that's all on one level. As well as terracing it to create flat areas, Joe's main idea was to design it on the diagonal. This makes a long thin garden seem much wider and also creates a sense of flowing movement through the space. There had been very narrow steps on one side originally. Instead, Joe created very broad, much more inviting steps, flanked by retaining walls made from new railway sleepers. The steps were infilled with gravel laid on top of a weed-suppressing membrane.

On the patio, Joe used some of the original Staffordshire blue bricks as a panel between areas of imitation York stone paving and, above it, made a pergola with 15 x 2.5cm (6 x 1in) planks slotting together to form a grid. Planted with the grapevine, *Vitis* 'Brant', this created a shady seating area, and framed the view of the garden from the back door.

At the top of these steps, on the first level, was the potager – four quadrant-shaped beds for herbs and vegetables. There were also runner beans growing in pots and climbing up copper obelisks. At the centre of the parterre was a circular, raised pool, rendered and painted warm yellow. In it, Rachel planted a small white water lily and, for a strong vertical accent, the striped rush, *Schoenoplectus* 'Zebrinus'.

In the course of restoring the garden, Joe discovered a natural spring which made part of the garden more or less permanently boggy. In line with their philosophy of working with nature, not fighting it, Rachel chose moisture-loving bog plants for that bed, including the dramatic *Darmera peltata*, with leaves up to 60cm (2ft) across.

Rachel bought some of the plants from a local garden centre, choosing her structural evergreens for the woodland area, such as *Sarcococca hookeriana* var. *digyna*, commonly known as the Christmas box (to go under the Christmas tree!), *Helleborus orientalis* and evergreen ferns. The rest of the plants were ordered on the Internet and delivered by van. Among the shrubs included was the deep yellow rose *Rosa* GOLDEN TRUST, named for the Bourneville Village Trust's centenary. Most of the other planting was herbaceous, to give impact in the first season. For drama towards the back of the border, Rachel chose tall architectural plants, such as the jagged-leafed bears' breeches, *Acanthus spinosus*, and *Lysimachia ciliata* 'Firecracker', with beetroot-red leaves and yellow flowers. There were also silvery artemisias, penstemons, and *Knautia macedonica*, which produces its maroon, clover-like flowers right through the summer.

At the open day towards the end of the summer, many visitors who knew the garden in the past were thrilled by the transformation. The Slater brothers, who had grown up there in the 30s and 40s, felt that their parents, who had loved the garden, would have been over the moon.

Tree Arches & Cloud Pruning

Ivan Hicks loves sculpting with trees, and one of the simplest forms he creates are tree arches. As he points out, the classic Gothic arch was formed originally by crossing two branches.

Plant two young trees such as silver birch, *Betula pendula* or rowan, *Sorbus aucuparia*, a door's width apart, then tie one branch from each together with a tree tie to form an arch above your head. In two or three years' time, remove the tree tie. You could make a pyramid with two pairs of trees planted in a square and tied together in the centre. Ivan's dislike of the Leyland cypress is well-known, but he puts them to good use planted to make first an arch, and then when the growth was strong and tall enough, to cut out a window above it .

CLOUD PRUNING

The Oriental art of cloud pruning is a form of topiary that is meant to simulate pine trees in the landscape. Although the topiary is available from specialist nurseries, it costs a fortune so, in 1999, Ivan Hicks demonstrated how to create your own. You need an evergreen shrub – something like box, *Buxus sempervirens*, or fast- growing shrubby honeysuckle,

Lonicera nitida, or even the distinctly fluffy and cloud-like conifer *Cryptomeria japonica* – with three or four main stems and plenty of side shoots on which to hang the 'clouds'. You may have a shrub growing in the garden already that's suitable, but if not, go and buy one from the garden centre. What you are looking for is a plant with a good internal structure, a good skeleton, so do push the outer growth out of the way and have a good look inside.

Ivan finds it easier to use scissors, rather than secateurs, to cut away the excess growth to leave you with the desired cloud shape. He also recommends stepping back fairly often to see what you've done and get an overall sense of the shape. You may find the shrub is too upright and the stems too close together when you have finished so, to separate them, twist wire around each stem, as you do with bonsai, and then bend them apart. In a year or two, you will be able to remove the wire.

Presenter 1989 – 1992

Nigel Colborn

After attending the Kings School in Ely, Nigel studied botany at Cornell University in USA. On his return to the UK, he worked in the animal nutrition industry before giving it up to become a farmer in Lincolnshire . He farmed for ten years, and only gave up his tenancy to become a full-time writer and broadcaster. He also developed a delightful garden at his home at Careby Manor in Lincolnshire and for a time, ran a small nursery selling the sort of specialist plants that he loved to grow.

It was as the result of a visit paid to the nursery by Geoff Hamilton and the *Gardeners' World* team in the late 1980s that Nigel was eventually invited to become a presenter on the programme . He's appeared on many other gardening programmes, such as BBC *Gardener of the Year* and *How Does Your Garden Grow* and has been a regular panellist on Radio 4's *Gardeners' Question Time* since the mid 1990s.

He has written a number of gardening books, among them *Short Cuts to Great Gardens*, *A Flower for Every Day* and *The Garden Floor*, as well as a humorous look at country life, *Family Piles,* and three novels. He also writes articles for a variety of newspapers and magazines, including *Gardeners' World Magazine*.

Nigel has been on the Royal Horticultural Society's Committee 'A' for some years, judging plant exhibits at shows, including the Chelsea Flower Show, something that keeps him very closely in touch with developments in plants and in garden design. In 2002, he was invited to join the RHS Council, a great honour in the gardening world. He is also a frequent guide on gardening cruises, something that not only allows him to travel to exotic places but also keeps him in touch with keen gardeners.

Presenter 1992 – 1995

Adrian Bloom

It is no surprise that Adrian Bloom has become one of the country's best known plantsmen. His father Alan, another great plantsman, now in his mid-nineties, founded the famous nursery Blooms of Bressingham in 1926 and Adrian grew up with plants in his blood. As well as working in the family firm, breeding and discovering new varieties from all over the world – there are many perennials particularly with 'Bloom' or 'Bressingham' in their name – Adrian was responsible for creating the firm's gold-medal-winning displays at the Chelsea Flower Show year after year. He also became an author and broadcaster. His television debut was with the young Geoff Hamilton in Anglia's *Gardening Diary* in 1971.

Once Geoff became the main presenter of *Gardeners' World*, Adrian also appeared as a guest expert at Barnsdale and, in 1992, became a regular, presenting a series of plant profiles.

Adrian was interested not just in individual plants, but in effective plant associations, long before it became fashionable, and his own six-acre garden Foggy Bottom, near Bressingham, is famous not only for its plantings of perennials and grasses, but also its all-year-round colour and its large collection of conifers. The garden, like The Dell, his father's equally famous garden next door, is open to the public.

Adrian holds the Royal Horticultural Society's coveted Victoria Medal of Honour (VMH) for service to horticulture, as does his father Alan. Only 63 people can hold the award at any one time (for the years of Queen Victoria's reign) and the Blooms are the only father and son ever to be honoured this way at the same time.

Large Gardens

Great Dixter

One of the greatest influences on the way we garden now is undoubtedly Christopher Lloyd, whose garden, Great Dixter, in East Sussex, is one of the great gardens of today. Not surprisingly, *Gardeners' World* has visited it many times.

Although he is now eighty-two, Christopher Lloyd is still one of the country's most adventurous gardeners still, with a passion for experiment and an eagerness to try new plants and combinations. The fact that so many of us are no longer frightened of using bright, bold colours in the garden is in large part due to him.

Christopher Lloyd was born in the house at Great Dixter, which his father, Nathaniel, had bought some ten years earlier in a rundown state . He invited Edwin Lutyens (the architect who designed the 'bones' of many Jekyll gardens) to oversee the restoration and design the garden.

Christopher took an interest in plants right from the start and was very lucky in his parents, who were both passionate gardeners. His father's interest was more architectural – the hard elements and structural planting, such as the hedges and the topiaries that are still one of Dixter's glories – while his mother was a great plantswoman.

He took a degree in horticulture at Wye College and lectured there for four years but, in 1954, after the death of his father, he came back to Great Dixter. Faced with the problem of making the place viable, he began to write

about gardening. His first book, *The Mixed Border*, appeared in 1957, to be followed over the years by many others, mostly still in print. He wrote a monthly column for *Country Life* for many years and still appears weekly in *The Guardian*. He started a nursery, specialising in clematis, but also selling other plants that he enjoys growing.

Christopher believes the big change came when Fergus Garrett came to join him at Great Dixter in 1992. They'd met when Fergus came to Dixter with a group of other students from Wye College and a friendship began. Some time later he asked Fergus to be his head gardener.

Christopher believes that where gardens are concerned two heads are better than one. 'It needs two of you to bounce ideas around. Not only do you get their ideas, but also you find that your own ideas flow more freely if you're talking with someone who knows what they're talking about. It's not good enough for the husband to say "Oh, I'm just the dogsbody." If you are an intelligent woman, you must have a garden-intelligent sort of a husband. If not, perhaps you should consider some sort of a change.'

The first major project after Fergus arrived was to convert the old Lutyens rose garden into a garden with a tropical feel in late summer with bananas, cannas and dahlias, all in vibrant colours. Christopher had become 'thoroughly bored' with the roses and, after eighty years, rose replant sickness meant that they just did not thrive any more. At the time, it caused some fluttering in the horticultural dovecotes, but it has proved to be hugely influential in the way that many of us garden.

Another of Dixter's great glories is the Long border – 33 x 4.5m (110 x 15ft) – which is the showcase and test bed for many of Christopher and Fergus's planting ideas, for example, plant combinations and the extensive use of annuals and half-hardy perennials to extend the flowering season.

Red is a colour that is always difficult to find in perennial plants, so they boost the border with dahlias like *D.* 'Grenadier' and a rose 'Florence Mary Morse', which has vivid scarlet flowers, with the tall white spires of cimicifuga growing in front of it. Although Christopher

ripped all the roses out of the rose garden, he feels they do have their uses. 'If you grow them in mixed borders, you don't get much in the way of pests and diseases.'

Strong colour contrasts is what Dixter has become known for in recent years, though Christopher doesn't understand why people find it difficult. 'Colour theming and harmony are all right as far they go, but you miss out on such a lot if you forget the contrasts. When I plant some contrasting combinations, some will say, "Oh Christopher Lloyd, he just wants to shock you with his contrasts!" But that's not true at all. I garden first and foremost to please myself, and if a colour contrast is exciting, I want to try it out.' So he will plant the warm brick-red *Helenium* 'Moerheim Beauty' with a bright mauve phlox, and the scrambling hardy geranium 'Anne Folkard', with its bright magenta, black-eyed flowers and lime green foliage, with *Euphorbia schillingii*, which has equally vivid lime green bracts.

Christopher loves the brilliant metallic blue of the sea holly, *Eryngium* x *oliverianum*, and thinks it needs something to set it off with a really bright colour, such as red or orange. 'There are nasturtiums growing nearby but they are so disobliging that they won't come as close to the eryngiums as I would like. They would look marvellous scrambling through it, but they are scrambling through something else instead.'

As Christopher grows only plants that he really likes, it is impossible for him to choose a favourite. ' The answer has to be "The one I am looking at at the moment." If it's a plant that I love, then I love it best because I'm looking at it and it's giving me pleasure.'

Colours at Great Dixter

Red The most dangerous colour of all, the one that causes fury – red rag to a bull.

Orange Probably the most exciting colour of all. Think of orange embers glowing in a fire.

Yellow A cheerful colour, the colour of sunlight, of warmth, of good cheer.

Green The colour of life. No green, no life.

Blue Everyone's colour, everybody adores blue. So many people say they grow only blue flowers in their garden.

Purple A sumptuous colour that suggests velvet. Have fun with it when it becomes magenta.

White Dazzling, it stands for purity, which is difficult to live up to.

The Garden House

For an exciting vision of the way gardening might develop in the future, The Garden House at Buckland Monachorum in Devon is the place to go.

Gardeners' World had visited several times over the years and, in 2000, Stephan Lacey made three visits to the garden to see how it developed through the seasons, while Alan Titchmarsh and Rachel de Thame paid their final visit in early summer 2001.

The original two-acre walled garden was developed between 1945 and 1981 by Lionel Fortescue, a retired Eton schoolmaster. It is a magnificent site on a north-west facing slope on the edge of Dartmoor, but not without its problems. It has twice the average rainfall, for example, and not a great deal of sun, so while moisture-lovers thrive, sun-lovers can struggle a bit.

The fact that the walled garden had been a vegetable garden for centuries and was limed regularly meant that it was impossible to grow lime-hating rhododendrons and camellias, and so it had to be herbaceous perennials. Lionel Fortescue was a great plantsman and grew only the very best forms and cultivars in the original garden, which was laid out very formally, with the plants well-tended, fed regularly and grown in neat blocks. In 1978, Keith Wiley came to work for Lionel Fortescue and, since the latter's death, has been the garden's guiding genius, seeing it expand into the countryside to cover ten acres. Part of what makes The Garden House so exciting is the contrast between the old and the new, between the formal – though the planting is now less formal than it once was – and the very informal and naturalistic. According to Stephan Lacey, Keith Wiley is probably the most adventurous and exciting gardener in Britain today. What makes him special is his genuine passion for landscape, whether it's the British Isles, Cretan wild flower meadows or the South African veldt, and his talent for extracting its essence – not simply copying it – and translating it to a garden setting.

It began initially because Keith kept seeing plants in the wild around the world and thinking that they bore no resemblance to the way we grow them in our gardens.

The landscape, he believes, is the most fantastic resource for gardening ideas that we're just not using yet. People who say there are no new ideas in gardening, Keith maintains, are talking rubbish! Keith's way with plants takes courage sometimes. *Magnolia stellata* is treated as ground cover, for example, cut hard back every year; and the vast carpets of thyme in the Cretan meadow are sheared annually to within a centimetre of their lives after flowering. With tall perennials like *Campanula lactiflora* and Michaelmas daisies, Keith waits until they are just about to flower then cuts them down to various heights. The result is very sturdy bushy new growth that doesn't need staking, and a staggered flowering time, which extends the season considerably.

The South African area is a riot of colour all summer long. Annuals are such wonderful plants, he says, but we've got used to growing them in such staid old ways! Why not just let them go? We think the natural habitat of *Petunia* 'Million Bells' is a hanging basket, but it grows happily in sandy places, and French marigolds, *Tagetes*, look wonderful in a jumble of other things. Before he went to South Africa he was asked why South African plants only flower for a very short time there but here, would flower all summer. The answer is that there, they grow in pure sand and have just enough energy to get out of the ground before the sun shrivels them up.

Here, Keith puts down a layer of compost first, then sand, so they think they're in England in their roots and South Africa in their tops! Not all the plants are South African –

many just won't grow in damper Devon – so he uses plants from regions with a similar climate, like California. Californian poppies, *Eschscholzia*, in brilliant burnt orange and pale yellow are a fantastic addition.

In autumn, some of the plants in this part of the garden are still blooming, but many have died and, while some people might think it looks a mess, Keith values the beauty of the seedheads for their contribution to the display. From mid-autumn onwards the plants are cut down selectively to allow the winter-seeding plants to germinate. When nothing's in flower, he tries to make the area look like a sculpture in sand, so that you get the magical idea later on of the flowering of the desert!

One of the newest areas at The Garden House is the prairie garden, inspired by the tall straight trunks of some thujas, revealed when a Leylandii hedge came out.

Along with tall grasses there are species Michaelmas daisies that give a dreamy wash of colour. While there are

some American plants, such as black-eyed Susan, *Rudbeckia fulgida*, and Joe Pye weed, *Eupatorium purpureum*, and grasses like *Panicum*, there are also Chinese grasses, like *Miscanthus sinensis* 'Silberfeder' and South American Pampas grass, *Cortaderia*, a classic suburban plant, used in a much more naturalistic setting.

The area is a natural slope but Keith has also moved vast amounts of soil to create even more contours so that grasses are growing above your head and make you feel that you really are a part of the garden.

When Keith first came to The Garden House, there were two gardeners looking after two acres. Now there are ten acres and only six gardeners, so he has had to adopt a new attitude to weeds. He began to see that they could look fantastic, growing with and through other plants in a community as they do in the wild. Visitors often tell him that they love The Garden House because it's the only garden they know that has more weeds than their own!

Audley End

Audley End, the magnificent Jacobean mansion near Saffron Walden built in 1603, was given to the nation in lieu of death duties just after the World War II. Like so many great country houses, it had become impossibly expensive to maintain, and had fallen into disrepair.

Work on restoring the gardens had begun some years ago and, in 1999, English Heritage and the Henry Doubleday Research Association (HDRA), began restoring the near-derelict two-acre walled Victorian kitchen garden. Chris Beardshaw followed the garden through a year with head gardener Mike Thurlow.

The restoration team at Audley End were lucky in finding some records of the kitchen garden in its heyday: a plan from 1877, for example, an order for fruit trees and the diary of one William Cresswell, journeyman gardener at Audley End during 1874.

August 1874 Friday 14th Wind SW, stormy, not much sun. Winter spinach sown on ground where spring cauliflowers were grown, having been well manured, dug up and firmly trod. Watered cucumber with manure water, afterwards with clean water to cleanse foliage.

The garden has been faithfully restored, but with one major difference. It is now gardened organically.

'While the Victorians used organic matter to keep the soil in good heart, as we do now,' said Mike Thurlow, 'they also used heavy-duty chemicals like lead and arsenic, to control pests and diseases. We grow mainly Victorian varieties of fruit and vegetables and not using chemicals hasn't caused many problems, so they could have been organic, too.'

October In the glasshouse, Mike collected tomato seeds for next year as Victorian head gardeners were expected to do. Having been given seeds of old varieties by the HDRA's Heritage seed library, Mike was keen to send some back. He stored carrots in a clamp. The carrots are piled neatly into a cone shape, which is covered first with a layer of straw, with a 'chimney' in the centre so that air can get in, then with soil. When Mike dug the carrots out in February, they were undamaged, still crunchy and full of flavour.

December One of the last jobs of the year was pruning the huge vines, some nearly 200 years old, in the restored vine houses. After pruning the spurs , they take the long growths down from their supports and lay them on the ground for the winter, partly to restrict the flow of sap, and partly to scrape all the pests off the bark. In March, they'll tie them back up again.

April The new box hedges, planted the previous year were due for their first cut. It's easier to cut box after it's been watered because the shears stay free of sap – rather like cutting hair when wet. The hedges have box blight and Mike finds watering them with dilute liquid seaweed doesn't cure it but helps the plants grow through it.

June In the orchard house, where stone fruit grows in pots, Mike shook the trees to assist the 'June drop' – when fruit trees naturally shed small immature fruits to allow the remainder to grow to a good size.

July Mike feels broad beans are underrated. The Victorians ate them young, as mange-tout and when they got old and tough, the servants had them, shelled. They do get attacked by blackfly, but ladybirds and their larvae see them off. If you interfere with the food chain, Mike says, the predators disappear and there's nothing to eat the pests when they return.

In Victorian times, when the family was at the London house, kitchen garden produce would be sent up to town every day by train. These days much of Audley End's produce makes the journey by van to the Dorchester Hotel where it features – by name – on the menu.

Abbey House

The Abbey House, Malmesbury, stands out in viewers' memories, partly because its owners, Ian and Barbara Pollard like to garden wearing the barest minimum – in his case, calf-length boots, a tool belt and a pink satin jock strap! It is also a magical garden.

Over the last seven years, they have transformed five weed-filled acres around a Tudor manor house built on the site of a medieval abbey in the middle of Malmesbury.

The house has a long, rich history dating back to the 7th century, when the Abbey was founded, becoming the third most important religious centre in England, after Canterbury and Winchester. How many gardens can boast both a saint and a king – Bishop Aldhelm, canonised in AD 720, and Athelstan, grandson of Alfred and the first king of all England – buried within their walls?

Rather than recreate a medieval garden, Ian has taken medieval elements, such as a herbarium, a vinery, a stew pond, and a 'pentice' (a covered monastic walkway) and used them as touchstones back to the past. The patterns of the knot garden at the front of the house, for instance, are based on a Celtic cross found on Iona, from where Maedulf, the monk who founded Malmesbury Abbey, originally came.

Ian trained as a chartered surveyor, not an architect; he has nonetheless designed and built some remarkable buildings, such as the Marco Polo by Battersea Park. But he never sat down and drew up a master plan for the garden. 'A sculptor doesn't impose the shape on the stone, the shape is already there in the stone and all he does is release it. That's how design here has evolved – organically.'

His professional skills and experience have been useful in other ways, though. Take the waterfall. 'I was wondering how to finish off this corner and thought "A twenty-foot waterfall would be quite nice". So I designed it and built it with the help of a gardener and digger driver. We built the first half of the horseshoe, then piled up fifty tons of scalpings to a height of six or seven feet to make a platform to finish it off – the way they built the pyramids. Then we took the scalpings down and spread them on the paths round the garden.'

His passion for plants came from developing his first great garden, the 180 acres of Hazelbury Manor, also in Wiltshire, and, while the Abbey House garden is much smaller, he still does things on a grand scale. He loves roses, so there are 2,200 different varieties of rose – and half a million dead heads every summer. He loves old varieties of fruit, so there are 180 of those, most of them cordons. Tulips too are a passion; there are 45,000 of them. He reckons they've spent about £300,000 on plants, but of course his labour is free, and he spends about twelve hours a day working in the garden. Like all proper gardeners, he never sits in the garden. 'In the way that kestrels in flight apparently see tiny rodents scuttling through the grass in bright yellow, I see weeds. We'll be looking at a beautiful border, and one little bit of bittercress will shine out bright yellow for me. I just have to get it out before it sets seed.'

Ian and Barbara love the garden so much they haven't had a holiday for five years, which is tough, he admits, on their three children. And he knows they will never, ever leave. 'This is a unique spot. We're here until the end and then they can throw us on the compost heap.'

Presenter 1992 – 1995

Liz Rigbey

Liz Rigbey's route to Gardeners' World was a somewhat circuitous one. Having read English at Exeter University, she embarked on a career in journalism that took her to *Farmers' Weekly*. From there it was a logical step to a reporter's job on Radio 4's early morning programme for farmers, *On Your Farm*. While she was there, she did an item on farming in the future in the form of a futuristic episode of *The Archers*, which was very well received. As a direct result, when the editorship of *The Archers* became vacant soon after, she applied for the job and got it. It was Liz who was responsible for the creation of the character of Lynda Snell.

Having become increasingly interested in gardening, by the late 1980s, Liz decided to change tack and took a course on garden design at Pershore College.

In 1991, she applied for a job as a researcher on the BBC 2 series *Dream Gardens*. She so impressed the production team that they asked her to present one of the programmes, *Gardens of the Mind*, for which she interviewed, among others, Ivan Hicks. In 1992, she joined Gardeners' World as a presenter, specialising in garden visits and interviews.

Towards the end of her time on the programme, she started writing her first novel, *Total Eclipse*, a psychological thriller that was published here and in the USA to great acclaim. Since then, she has worked as a broadcasting consultant in both Russia and Kenya, helping to start educational radio soap operas, which is how *The Archers* had started life and, in 2002, published her second novel, *Summertime*.

Presenter 1992 – 2002

Stephan Lacey

Stephan became interested in plants and gardens while he was surrounded by beautiful examples as a student at Oxford, where he started reading law but then switched to modern languages – French and German. For five years after he graduated, he worked in property investment in the City, while becoming more and more passionate about gardens and, indeed, taking over his parents' garden in North Wales to put his ideas into practice. In the mid '80s he decided to forge a new career in gardening.

He felt that, with no horticultural qualifications, the best way to launch himself as a garden writer was with a bang – a book rather than with the odd magazine or newspaper article. So he wrote the first few chapters of what was to be the highly acclaimed 'The Startling Jungle' on his kitchen table, and as a result found a publisher.

That led to a regular contributions to *The Daily Telegraph* Saturday gardening pages and eventually to television.

He made his television gardening debut in 1991 in the series *Dream Gardens*, presenting a programme from Monet's garden in Giverny with novelist and painter Molly Parkin. He soon became a regular on Gardeners' World, specialising in visits to larger gardens. He also presented strands within the programme on scent, on colour from Kiftsgate and planting for autumn colour from Powis Castle.

He has written several more highly regarded gardening books, including *Gardens of the National Trust* and most recently, *Real Gardening*. He continues to contribute regularly to the *Daily Telegraph* on the Saturday gardening pages, and is great demand in the USA as well as this country as a lecturer. At present, he gardens in London on a very small balcony. Having sold his late parents' house, he has moved the garden – trees, greenhouse and all – to his brother's home while he takes the time to decide where he wants to make his next proper garden.

Gardeners' World
Abroad

Hanami

Between January and May each year on Japanese television, they don't just have the weather forecast every night, they have the cherry blossom forecast, reporting on where the blossom will be at its best the following day. Cherry blossom is deeply significant in Japanese culture as a symbol of spring, of returning life and energy, and *Hanami* – viewing the cherry blossom – is a very important ritual in Japanese life. By day people stroll along admiring the trees and at night, they gather for somewhat less reverential parties under the trees at which large quantities of *sake* are drunk.

In April 1998, Gay Search visited Maruyama Park in Kyoto, world-famous for its cherry trees. One of the most spectacular trees in the park, a huge white cherry, was planted about one hundred years ago by the father of Touremon Sano. He is known in Japan as 'Mr Cherry Blossom', and is the owner of the largest flowering cherry nurseries in the country.

Today he still travels all over Japan, trying to conserve old cherry trees, to propagate from them and to discover new hybrids in the wild. What he does not do is hybridise trees himself. 'Morally I am against it. Cherries should seed themselves naturally through the birds and the insects. You should not break the rhythm of the natural world.'

TEMPLE GARDEN

Although in the West we think that Japanese gardens involve rocks, gravel and very few plants, a visit to Kyoto, the ancient capital of Japan, reveals that there are other styles. The temple of Toji-in has its dry landscape garden , but there is also a strolling garden which, in high contrast, is densely planted with carefully clipped, mainly evergreen trees and shrubs. A path of unevenly placed stepping stones leads you around a pond – the unevenness is deliberate, to make you watch where you put your feet. Then, when you reach even ground, you look up and see the view that has been carefully composed for you.

Traditional Japanese gardens are instant, planted with mature specimens, which are then clipped and trained to stay the same size. Green is the predominant colour, though there are splashes of other colours – for example, the scarlet of cotoneaster berries and camellia flowers, the pink of cherry blossom. 'The flower colour is important,' said Kowakatsu-san, the gardener-monk in charge of the garden, 'to give you a sense of the seasons. I have only seen photographs of European gardens, but they seem to me to be far from nature. A Japanese garden tries to blend with nature, to form part of the natural landscape. If you look at this garden it is hard to tell where it ends and the mountain begins.'

Green Guerrillas

In 1973, New York artist Liz Christy was tired of looking at a squalid, rubbish-filled vacant lot in her neighbourhood on the Lower East Side of Manhattan and decided to take it over, initially without permission, and make it into a community garden.

And so the Green Guerrilla movement was born and now, thirty years on, there are hundreds of similar gardens all over Manhattan, many of them temporary, using land until it is needed for redevelopment, but some are permanent. The original space, on the corner of East Houston and the Bowery, then Manhattan's 'ultimate slime spot' and otherwise known as Skid Row, measured 15 x 60m (50 x 200ft) and in the first year, Liz and her fellow volunteers shifted between eighty and a hundred bags of rubbish each week.

'When we started here,' volunteer Don Loggins told Liz Rigbey in 1993, 'we didn't realise that the subway was right below us. So we dug down six or eight feet to plant a tree and hit rock, so we broke through the rock, looked down and there were lights and people waiting on the platform looking up at us, wondering what on earth was going on. We put the rocks back, and moved the tree a little further in.'

By the time Liz Rigbey visited the garden it was twenty years old and very well established, a remarkably leafy and tranquil green oasis amid the hustle and bustle of the city streets. They grow not just ornamental plants, like climbing roses and Virginia creeper over what were once graffiti-covered walls, but also edible crops such as figs, grapes, peaches and even rhubarb, which ends up in pies or ice-cream.

There is a remarkable amount of wildlife too, given that the garden is surrounded by busy city streets. In the pond, there are frogs, turtles and goldfish. The gardeners always enjoyed seeing the puzzled expressions on the faces of passers by who couldn't believe they were

hearing frogs on the Lower East Side. And from the bee hives on top of the shed they harvest around 90kg (200lbs) of honey a year.

There is a downside. Theft is a problem so anything portable – wheelbarrows or even some shrubs and trees – is chained down. 'This can be a little demoralising sometimes, but the feedback we get from the public gives us a very good feeling.'

Westpark

If the words 'public park' conjure up in your mind little but carpet bedding and roses growing in bare soil, then Westpark in Munich will undoubtedly make you think again.

Created just over twenty years ago from a disused gravel pit, it is now one of the finest perennial and grass gardens in Europe, as Stephan Lacey discovered when he visited twice, first in the autumn of 1994 and again in high summer 1995.

What makes it such a revolutionary approach to planting and maintenance is that the plants aren't arranged in separate blocks or tiered from front to back. They are planted according to natural rhythms, some in loose drifts others standing alone and being repeated as they would be in the wild. But, as Stephan pointed out, while the inspiration comes from the wild, this is no superficial mimicry of nature.

The perennial garden is divided into three different areas – a rock garden, a more moisture-retentive meadow/woodland fringe area and dry meadowland or steppe – and only those plants that are naturally adapted to those conditions are planted there, regardless of their geographical origins.

The plants at Westpark are never fed or watered so they don't grow unnaturally large or lush and therefore don't need staking, lifting or dividing. They are also less likely to fall victim to pests and diseases. The plants used are carefully chosen, with any thugs excluded, and then are left to get on with it. They are grown hard so they can cope with extremes of weather. They self seed as in the wild, and move around into new areas, so all the gardeners have to do is some deadheading, a bit of weeding and very occasionally, troubleshooting.

Not that there's much deadheading because the seedheads of alliums, irises, asphodelines, sedums and so on, are very much part of the display. As Stephan put it, 'The natural aesthetic of Westpark means that, like on a country walk, you don't think "How messy!" You accept the natural processes of decay and the gaps as all contributing to the picture.'

There is not much weeding either, partly because the planting is dense and also because the deliberately low fertility of the soil does not encourage weeds.

It is not a one-season garden by any means. It looks wonderful in spring, summer and autumn and, in fact, is designed to reach a flowering climax every three weeks in summer.

What makes Westpark such an inspiration is that it plugs into so many of the current gardening trends. It's ecological, it's labour-saving, it reflects the growing interest in wild plants, a more relaxed style of gardening, and an appreciation of the beauty of stems and seedheads. Stephan Lacey ended his report with a plea for our public parks to take a leaf from Westpark's book, but some years on, apart from some developments in Sheffield, there is little to suggest the days of the bedding and roses are over.

Maria Hofker

Like many people who live in Amsterdam, the artist Maria Hofker did her gardening not at home but in her *volkgarten*, a kind of allotment complete with summerhouse, a twenty-minute bicycle ride from the city.

She was ninety when Liz Rigbey visited her in 1992 (she died in December 1999), but was still avidly gardening and painting the plants that she grew there.

She had started keeping a journal of the garden illustrated with her beautiful water colours soon after the Second World War. She and her husband, Willem, also an artist, had lived and painted in Bali for years but, during the war, were prisoners of the Japanese and returned home empty-handed in 1945 with nothing to show for all their years there. That experience made her determined to keep a record of her life in her garden.

As a painter, she said, she always looked at the colour of a plant first, and especially loved soft yellows, and all kinds of pinks and purples. 'For one year I had bright red poppies, with just one purple one, so I saved the seeds of that and now virtually all the red ones have gone.' Her passions were roses and thistles.

She loved roses for their shape, for their range of colours and their scent – she couldn't see the point of a rose without scent – and did many drawings and paintings of them. In 1992, a yellow rose was named after her in Holland.

She loved all kinds of thistles, a less obvious choice perhaps, but for the same reasons – the shape of the jagged leaves and the flower, and their rich blue-purple colour. 'I saw one in Sissinghurst once, with wonderful purpley-blue flowers, and there was one flower head lying on the floor, so I picked it up, brought it home and drew it.

The seeds did nothing, though. We have a saying in Holland, "When you take something you are not allowed to, it does not succeed."' Maria Hofker's gardening rule was very simple: 'Give the plant what the plant likes. Foxgloves need half-shade, so give them half shade.'

Her garden gave her pleasure and inspiration all through the year, even, as she said, in the rain and the wind and, when there were no flowers to paint, she drew seedheads, stems, berries.

'It would be impossible to live without my garden because it is nature and nature is in everybody. I need it so much – to hear the wind in the poplar trees, to smell the roses. As an artist, I can't imagine living without nature.'

Gardeners' World Abroad 135

Presenter 1993 – 1995

Nick Wray

Nick, who never wanted to be anything but a gardener, had been superintendent of the University of Bristol's Botanical Garden for just a year when he was interviewed by Geoff Hamilton during the making of his series *The Living Garden* in the summer of 1992. Geoff was very impressed with Nick's contribution to the programme and knowing the production team was looking for new younger talent, suggested him as a presenter for Gardeners' World.

Nick's role in the programme was that of roving interviewer rather than practical gardener and his interviewees ranged from Nicholas de Rothschild at Exbury, talking about the superbly fragrant Exbury hydrid azaleas to 'Sid the Pink', Sid Hall, a Nottinghamshire miner who spent his spare daylight hours growing and breeding pinks (*Dianthus*) in his back garden. Nick's outstanding memory of the

programme is a trip he made to South Africa in 1994, which took in not only the world famous Kirstenbosch Botanical Gardens but a vegetable garden in a township.

Although Nick made many appearances on Gardeners' World, he was never tempted to give up the day job for a full-time career in broadcasting. After he left the series in 1995, he appeared on HTV's *Garden Calendar* from time to time but, for the last few years, has concentrated all his efforts on the botanical garden in Bristol. Its current site, in Clifton, is to be sold, and having successfully made the case to the university for keeping a botanical garden, Nick is now facing the prospect in the next two years of digging up the whole garden and moving it to a new site. With administration now taking up much of his working day, gardening is something he does at home for pleasure.

Bob Flowerdew

Organic gardener Bob Flowerdew always provoked very strong feelings in the audience. Some viewers loved his full-on approach to organic fruit and vegetable growing (indeed there is even a thriving Bring Back Bob Campaign on the internet demanding his return to Gardeners' World), while others found the use of old tyres, black polythene and defunct freezers in the garden as well as the waist-length plait a bit hard to take. Few people were indifferent to him.

Bob Flowerdew – another of those perfect horticultural names – was born into a family that has farmed in East Anglia since pre-Elizabethan times. Initially, though, Bob turned his back on the family farming tradition by taking a degree in financial management and working in the City before giving it up to work his way through Europe and North America, learning about different approaches to gardening and farming. He so enjoyed picking grapes with one French family that he returned for the harvest for twelve successive years. He also worked at a number of unlikely jobs rangng from chicken giblet washer to life model.

He finally settled on his plot near Diss in Norfolk sixteen years ago and since then has produced virtually every edible crop that will grow in this country, including pineapples and guavas. Ornamental plants have little place in his garden as he sees absolutely no point in growing anything he can't eat.

He also keeps chickens, ducks and geese, which not only provide eggs and eventually meat, but play a useful part in pest control and manure production, and he also keeps bees.

He's still a regular panellist on Radio 4's *Gardeners' Question Time*, has written a number of books on organic fruit and vegetable growing , the most recent being *The No Work Garden*. He runs a consultancy, teaches at a local college and lectures on organic gardening to groups all over the country.

The Nation's
Favourite Gardens

Sissinghurst

This is one of the most famous gardens in the world, so naturally Gardeners' World had long wanted to film there. For many years, however, the National Trust refused to allow the cameras in. It felt that the garden was already filled to bursting with visitors and television coverage would attract even more.

In 1995, the National Trust celebrated its centenary and, as part of the celebrations, *Gardeners' World* planned a series of films about the work of its head gardeners. With a new timed ticket system of entry at Sissinghurst keeping visitor numbers to a more manageable level, the Trust agreed that head gardener, Sarah Cook, could be among them.

Sissinghurst was the creation of Vita Sackville-West and her husband, Harold Nicolson, who bought the near-derelict castle, near Cranbourne in Kent, in 1930. They spent the next thirty-two years, until Vita's death in 1962, making a magnificent garden, or rather series of gardens, because although the site covers six acres, it is divided into smaller, more intimate spaces, just right for a family.

The Rose Garden is at its peak in June, when many of the old-fashioned varieties, which do not repeat, are in flower. In the Herb Garden, much of the colour in June comes from medicinal and dye plants, such as scarlet bergamot, *Monarda*, and bright yellow dyer's greenweed, *Genista tinctoria*, rather than culinary herbs. 'You have to be a bit careful with the drug plants,' Sarah remarked. 'Many of the leaves are poisonous, so don't just go round a herb garden picking and eating at will.'

The Cottage Garden, with its now-fashionable 'hot' colours, often comes as a shock to first-time visitors to Sissinghurst, who imagine it's all about muted tones and tasteful pastels. Keeping the reds, oranges and yellows all together, Sarah believes, is a very good way of using them in the garden. While the Rose Garden and the Cottage Garden have their fans, the White Garden, with its beds edged with neatly clipped box and planted with white flowers, is what most people associate with Sissinghurst. The central arbour, smothered in the single white flowers of *Rosa mulliganii* must be one of the most frequently photographed garden features in the world.

White gardens – indeed single colour gardens generally – have become very fashionable. 'The secret," said Sarah 'is to keep it not as quite as single colour as you think, so you've got lots of different green foliages, grey foliage and different shades of white. You need to very careful with that – if you put a blue white next to a yellow white, they can both wind up looking dirty. It's thinking as much about leaf shape and leaf textures as about the flowers.' Sarah and her team enjoy meeting the visitors who come from all over the world, but with one reservation. While people no longer take cuttings from the garden, some were still taking seedheads – distressing because attractive ones like *Nigella* and poppy prolong the display and also provide the seed to sow next year.

Sarah doesn't believe Sissinghurst should be a museum. 'While I don't think we have Vita and Harold sitting on our shoulders saying "Do this" or "Don't do that", the idea is to keep the philosophy behind it, to grow the types of plants that Vita and Harold would like. Obviously we'll keep the White Garden white and the Cottage Garden as hot colours, but part of Vita and Harold's pleasure in gardening was trying things out and so, if the garden wasn't alive like that, it wouldn't be Sissinghurst any more.'

Where is it?
Sissinghurst Garden, Cranbrook, Kent.
See the website www.nationaltrust.org.uk

Heligan

The nation's favourite garden, or rather gardens – by a long way – were the Lost Gardens of Heligan, near St Austell in Cornwall, although, with over three hundred and fifty thousand visitors each year, they hardly qualify as 'lost' any more. Coming top in the poll was an accolade that delighted the presiding genius behind the restoration of this eighty-acre site, Tim Smit.

He had originally trained as an architect but had had a very successful career in the 1980s as a record producer. At the end of that decade, he had moved down to Cornwall and found Heligan. 'On the morning of 16 February 1990, we cut our way with machetes into the citrus house, as it now is, and found this old vine still growing through the broken glass and the brambles. I just had a funny feeling that I had to restore it, and by the evening of that day I had decided to change career.'

The gardens, which had been superb during Victorian times had, like so many great gardens, gone into decline after the First World War. Almost anyone else would have been daunted by the sheer scale of the task, but Tim Smit relishes a challenge and decided to tackle it an area at a time. 'The first garden we broke into was the Italian garden. The laurel hedges were fifty feet in each direction so we cut them right down to stumps and found a wonderful wrought iron gate buried in among them, so we decided to do the Italian garden first.' Other gardens followed – the woodland garden, the rock garden, the magnificent kitchen garden, consisting of four walled gardens in which they now grow over three hundred varieties of fruit, vegetables and herbs.

'One of the things you find when you restore a place like this is that the rigour that drove people to produce to a quality goes if it's just a theme park. So we decided to make the vegetable garden produce for the restaurant, so that the cook could say, "That's not good enough", and keep the gardeners on their mettle. And if the flowers on the tables don't look good enough, we've got to grow them better. It's an integrated project.'

One of the last areas to be restored was the thirty-acre Lost Valley which, after over two thousand self-sown sycamore and ash trees had been carefully removed, revealed a jungle filled with subtropical plants. 'There's almost a mile-long avenue of tree ferns, *Dicksonia antarctica*, which came over on boats from New South Wales and are between three and four hundred years old – they almost humble you with their age. We also have a specimen of the only New Zealand yew which is capable of being turned into a war canoe.' Tim's own favourite spot in the garden, unexpectedly perhaps, is the potting shed in the melon yard, the oldest of the walled gardens. 'I don't know what it is about pine tables with zinc, compost mixing things, cut flowers, lots of sweet peas, vegetables, terracotta pots stacked against the wall, the tools, sisal … it just reeks of everything gardening means to me. I spend hours in there.'

What he thinks appeals so much to many of the visitors about Heligan (the Cornish word for willow, incidentally) is that it isn't grand. "There is nothing aristocratic about it that would make people think they couldn't have in a slightly shrunken form perhaps in their own garden. That's why people feel comfy here.'

Given the huge success of Heligan, it's no surprise that Tim Smit is now treated as a major authority on the restoration of great gardens. His views on the subject are somewhat surprising, however. 'It's a disease in Britain that people want to preserve and restore everything without judging its merit. I remember making a few people sit bolt upright at a meeting of the Historic Houses Association by saying, "If you can't make love in it, dream in it or get drunk in it, then for Gods' sake, tarmac it!"'

Tim's next project after Heligan was just down the road in a disused chalk pit – the phenomenally successful Eden Project, which attracted two million visitors in its first year. No doubt that will be topping the list of the nation's favourite gardens in the future.

Where is it?
Heligan Gardens, Pentewan, St Austell, Cornwall.
See the website www.heligan.com

Helen Dillon's Garden

Helen Dillon is Ireland's equivalent to Alan Titchmarsh or Monty Don – the country's No 1 TV gardening presenter on RTE's *Garden Heaven* – although neither of those two have been filmed gardening in dungarees and pearls.

Her garden in the Dublin suburb of Ranelagh is as famous there as Barnsdale or Barleywood here, since it's not only seen on television but Helen also opens it to the public.

She's been making the garden for thirty years now, but two years ago, she told Alan Titchmarsh, that she felt she'd become the curator of a museum.' I was just looking after what I had created – all I was doing was dusting and polishing.' So in a radical redesign, the large central lawn went, to be replaced by an elegant formal canal, flanked with near-white limestone paving. 'People who don't like it tell me it's 'challenging', while others reassure me it will tone down in time. I don't want it to tone down. In winter instead of gloomy green grass, the water shines and sparkles and glistens and is endlessly exciting.'

Helen Dillon divides gardeners into collectors and makers of garden pictures or, to put it another way, plantsmen and women as opposed to gardeners. In her own case, she finds it impossible to decide which she is. 'For one minute I'm thinking, "What an adorable little plant", and the next I'm screwing up my eyes and looking out the window and wanting to see a pretty picture. The two do not go together, so I am permanently in a filthy temper.'

As she gets older, however, she thinks she is tending more towards the making of garden pictures. She's still tries the smart, challenging plants, but if they're not happy in her garden, out they go. She likes common plants more and more and will accept plants that do a job for her, even if she doesn't altogether approve of them. 'The rose "Trumpeter" is a ferocious, ghastly horror, but it is a wonderful provider of terrific colour.'

Helen is delighted to share her garden with the many visitors who come and really doesn't care whether they are knowledgeable gardeners or not. 'I want people to go round, without knowing a single plant name, and say, "This makes me feel good. This calms me down. This is peaceful." Plants are the only tranquilliser that works.'

Where is it?
45 Sandford Road, Ranelagh, Dublin 6, Ireland.
Helen Dillon's garden is open to the public from: 2–6pm daily in March, July and August and on Sundays only in April, May, June and September.
See the website www.dillongarden.com

Lamorran

Lamorran House Garden, in St Mawes, Cornwall, has been created by Robert Dudley-Cook over the last twenty years. Originally half an acre round the house, it now extends to four acres, reclaimed from wilderness, of superbly designed gardens with Japanese and Mediterranean themes.

It is densely planted with many rare, subtropical plants, and with gravel paths and water threaded throughout. 'I sometimes describe it as an intestinal garden,' Robert Dudley-Cook said, 'because that's what the plan looks like. Visitors often say they can't believe it's only four acres because they feel they've walked miles.'

One viewer who nominated Lamorran was Sue Feldman from Nottingham. She had a fascinating story to tell about her discovery of the garden some years ago, and paid a return visit for the programme.

Ten years ago, she and her husband were in St Mawes on holiday and had stopped to admire some planting when an old man approached them in the street and asked if they'd like to see an interesting garden. They followed him along some very narrow paths and eventually *under* a gate. 'It did seem a very unusual way to visit a garden,' said Sue, 'but we were on holiday.'

The circumstances may have been surreal, but Sue was overwhelmed by what she saw. 'It's impossible to describe the garden's physicality. You are immediately part of it, immersed in the most incredible planting and it stimulates all your senses. As you walk this labyrinth of paths, you turn a corner and it's one joy after another. And what made that day even more special was our guide, whose knowledge of the plants was just phenomenal.'

Their guide on that surreal expedition, it turned out, wasn't Robert Dudley-Cook, but a local eccentric who regularly showed visitors round the garden, implying, but never actually saying, that it was his own.

'He could be exceedingly trying,' says Robert, 'but he loved the garden and was a mine of information on subtropical plants. He had no family, so after he died, we buried his ashes under one of our palm trees.'

Ten years ago, Sue described the garden as 'awesome'. Now, she calls it 'magnificent'.

Where is it?
Lamorran, Upper Castle Road, St Mawes, Cornwall.
See the website www.gardensincornwall.co.uk

White Gates

Obviously most of the gardens that featured among the nation's favourites are the large, famous ones open to the public, because thousands of visitors get to see them every year. Judy Beba-Thompson's tiny back garden, just outside Derby is also open to the public, though she can only accommodate one medium-sized busload at a time.

Judy, like over three thousand other garden owners all over the country, opens for charity under the National Gardens Scheme on a few Sundays during the summer months each year, and by appointment at other times. While keen gardeners love to admire large gardens, it's from less-than-average-sized plots like Judy's – it's only 5 x 12m (17 x 38ft) – that so many get most inspiration.

Judy's garden, designed for tranquillity and seclusion and richly planted for scent and colour, is divided into two sections. 'If you divide a small space, it makes it seem bigger because you can't see it all at once.'

The first area is romantic and pretty, in mainly pastel shades, with peonies, lilies, geraniums, clematis and roses. 'I started the garden because I wanted flowers to cut for the house, so I planted one rose bush. Now I have eighty-five.'

She loves old roses and has many 'French ladies', such as 'Madame Alfred Carriere', Madame Hardy' and 'Adelaide d'Orléans'. There is also a raised lily pond and a fountain, adding the calming sound of moving water.

Through a gothic arch, smothered in yet more roses, is the white garden, planted to be serene and calming. 'I'd read about such a thing, though I'd never actually seen one, and I knew it had to be something special. It is white, though there are one or two touches of pink but I tell myself they're white.' This too has its lily pond, small enough to hold a dwarf lily – white naturally.

The big difference between small gardens and large ones, Chris Beardshaw pointed out, is that in large gardens there is plenty of space so if a plant doesn't perform very well, there are still plenty of other things to look at. In small gardens, every plant has to earn its keep or it gets chucked out.

The visitors certainly love Judy's garden. 'It's packed full of treasures,' said one, while another found it inspirational. 'It shows how you can break up even a very small garden.'

Where is it?
For details of this and other gardens open for charity under The National Gardens Scheme, see the famous "Yellow Book" *Gardens of England and Wales Open for Charity*.
See the website www.ngs.org.uk

Filming at Barleywood

On filming days at Barleywood, usually the Friday before transmission, the team arrives at Alan's garden around 8.30 in the morning – the cameraman, soundman, executive producer, director, production assistant , and any of the other presenters needed on the day. The first job, apart getting the kettle on in the potting shed, is to get all the camera gear to the top of the garden – not just the camera and sound recording equipment but sometimes tracks on which the camera moves for long, smooth moving (tracking) shots, and sometimes a jib arm to swing the camera high off the ground – no mean feat when you consider the angle of the gradient.

Although film crews are all freelance, and shoot a whole range of different programmes, Gardeners' World has its team of regulars. As executive producer Colette Foster said, "It takes a particular skill to make plants look beautiful on film."

Colette will have been in constant touch with Alan during the previous week deciding on what he will do in the programme. Obviously they may have made plans earlier, but plants have minds of their own, and if it's too soon or too late to feature a particular plant, they have to find

something else to feature. While the cameraman is setting up for the first shot of the day, the producer and/or director talk through the running order with Alan and the other presenters. Meanwhile the sound recordist 'mic's up' everyone who is to speak – fits them with a small transmitter that slips into a back pocket, conceals the wires and clips on a very small radio mic' that is usually hidden under clothing, though sometimes if a fabric rustles too much, it may have to show.

Filming is always a slow process because every change of shot in a finished item has involved a new set-up, with the camera being moved. And of course things can go wrong; occasionally presenters get their words in a muddle or drop something. More often though, it is extraneous noise: the neighbour's mower, an ice cream van, dustbin collection day and, most common of all, aircraft noise. Filming with Gardeners' World, you realise that there is nowhere quiet left in Britain.

Frequent breaks for tea or coffee are essential to warm the hands as well as the inner person, as it can get very cold standing about outside. Filming continues in more or less all weathers. Unless the rain is torrential, you don't see it on camera and sometimes, when, for example, there is no alternative filming day available before transmission, filming continues even then. Alan always has a spare set of clothing that he wears for filming to cover such eventualities so that he can nip inside, get dry, change into dry clothes, put the wet stuff in the tumble drier and carry on filming.

Filming carries on until the light goes and then all the 'rushes' – the tapes shot that day – go back to base where, over the next few days, they are edited to length, the close-ups added, and music chosen ready for transmission.

Gay Search

Having read English at university, Gay was working as a freelance magazine journalist and author when she acquired her first garden – two-thirds of an acre of almost perfect soil in West Sussex – and the gardening bug bit. What started as a hobby, over the next few years gradually became her career.

Gay was writing a regular column on gardening for beginners in *Woman* magazine (as she had no horticultural qualifications , a young lad from Ilkley – one Alan Titchmarsh – used to check her copy to make sure she wasn't saying anything daft), when she met Geoff Hamilton in the mid 1980s. He eventually invited her to join him on a new series he was about to make called *First Time Garden*, turning a typical rubble-filled mud patch behind a house on a brand new estate in

Birmingham into a garden. They made two more series together, *First Time Planting*, filmed at Barnsdale, and *Old Garden, New Gardener*.

Gay went on to devise and present *Front Gardens*, perhaps the first of the garden design make-over programmes, and *More Front Gardens*, before becoming a member of the Gardeners' World team. Her speciality was quick and easy projects for new gardeners, such as the *Garden in a Season* (see page 102), as well as interviews with owners of small gardens.

Gay has written over twenty gardening books, the most recent being *The Impatient Gardener*. She was gardening editor of *Radio Times* and has been gardening editor of Sainsbury's Magazine since its first issue ten years ago.

Ivan Hicks

As much an artist as he is a gardener, Ivan was the programme's resident eccentric. Trained as an arboriculturist and horticulturist, he spent fifteen years as Head Gardener/Manager of the 35-acre garden at West Dean near Chichester owned by the wealthy surrealist and patron of the arts, the late Edward James. While he was there, he developed the garden attached to his tied cottage within the estate in what has become his own individual style.

Just after he left West Dean to go freelance in 1991, he was approached by Catalyst Television to feature in the 'Gardens of the Mind' episode of the series *Dream Gardens*, and, as he no longer had a garden of his own, they gave him £500 to create a new one especially for the programme in just over four months. He advertised for a garden in which to work, and was lucky enough to be

offered the use of an empty half-acre walled garden at Stanstead House in West Sussex. He named it 'The Garden In Mind' and over the next twelve years, it developed into a remarkable garden much admired for its art, its wit and humour, as well as Ivan's remarkable talent for shaping plants. Sadly, despite protests from leading garden historian Sir Roy Strong and the Garden History Society, The Garden in Mind is no more. It has just been demolished and replaced with a maze.

Ivan is currently working for a number of private clients, including butterfly fanatic and property developer Colin Farrell. Together they are developing plans for an enormous butterfly garden under a two-acre geodesic dome, alongside a garden festival focusing on modern design and lasting months rather than days, rather like the famous modern garden festival at Chaumont in France.

Gardeners' World
On Show

Shows

While the BBC has covered the Chelsea Flower Show since the 1950s, those programmes were made independently of *Gardeners' World*, although then as now, the presenters of the series also featured in the Chelsea coverage.

From time to time in the late '80s and '90s, when the main Chelsea coverage was one 50-minute programme midweek, which couldn't possibly cover everything, *Gardeners' World* did visit the show . But since then, there has been virtually wall-to-wall coverage, with Channel 4 from 1998 to 2000, and with the BBC from 2001 onwards, so there has been no need for *Gardeners' World* to have a presence, too.

As for the other major shows that sprang up in the 1990s, *Gardeners' World* has been there from the start. First there was the Hampton Court Palace Flower Show from 1990 and, from 1992, *Gardeners' World* Live! at the National Exhibition Centre in Birmingham – a spin-off from the magazine which, in turn, was a spin-off from the programme.

The first show featured as a ten-minute item within *Gardeners' World* since, editorially, there was not enough material to sustain a whole programme. But the amount of coverage grew year by year and by the late '90s it filled the whole half hour. For the last few years, it has been an hour-long special. The most recent show to take its place on the summer calender is Tatton Park.

But it's not just the grand and famous shows that have featured on *Gardeners' World* over the years. Many small, specialist, even quirky, local shows have featured too.

DAFFODILS

Ten years ago, carpenter Steve Holden from West Sussex, entered his first daffodil competition and was hooked. Now he grows over two hundred and fifty varieties and enters all the major shows during the season, from March to May. 'The National Daffodil Show happens at the end of April, and is geared more to growers in the Midlands and the north and we southerners have a struggle to do well there because that's very late in the season for us. So we think of the South of England Show at Tonbridge in Kent in mid-April as our "nationals".'

Gardeners' World joined him three days before the South of England Show in 2000, when he was finalising his choice of blooms for the competition.

What makes a good show daffodil? If you draw an imaginary line from twelve o'clock to six o'clock on the face of the flower, either side of the line should be identical. There should be no nicks or creases in the petals, it should have a good stem, the flower at ninety degrees to the stem, a good colour, and it should just shout "Look at me!"'

Once Steve has selected his blooms, there is no guarantee that they will reach the show bench unscathed. One of his 'Yellow-red' daffodils had been nibbled by earwigs and one of his Division 4 Double daffodils was suffering from 'greenback' – a green stripe up the back of the white petals. 'I put the stem in warm water, stand it by a warm radiator and change the water every few hours, and most of it has gone.' Another couple of blooms had problems with perianths (outer petals) curving backwards, and a piece of cardboard put behind them until the very last minute would do the trick. At the show, Steve always tries to get a spot in the centre of the bench for his display. 'The judges walk up and down, and if it's in the centre they'll really see it, whereas if it's on the end, they'll only see it once or twice.'

Steve's exhibit in the class for ten different daffodils, displayed in two vases of five blooms, won him first prize and the Ted Osbourne Memorial Trophy. 'If I didn't win anything, I would still do it because they are such lovely people at the shows and we have such fun.'

GOOSEBERRIES

Gooseberry growing, as a popular competitive sport, began in England in the 1750s, mainly among the weavers of Lancashire and Yorkshire who had room in their small back gardens for a bush or two. It continues to this day and, although the number of shows has declined since the First World War, those like the Olde Egton Bridge Gooseberry Show in North Yorkshire are still going strong.

The competitive classes of gooseberries are determined by colour. There's Red, with 'Lord Derby' one of the most

popular variety; Yellow, with 'Woodpecker' and 'Firbob'; White, with 'Katheryn Harley', one of the most successful varieties, and finally Green, where 'Surprise' is popular.

The beauty of this competition as opposed to other flower or produce shows is that, as one contestant put it, the scales are the only judge. There's no room for judges' personal likes and dislikes or politics. The heaviest gooseberry in each category wins and the heaviest gooseberry of all is the overall champion. It's as simple as that.

In 1993, when *Gardeners' World* paid a visit, the winner of the cup for the heaviest berry was a yellow 'Woodpecker', weighing in at 28 grammes 12 grains. Even gooseberry shows have gone metric, although the majority of the competitors, who are of a certain age, still think in ounces, so in imperial that's just about one ounce.

Every grower has his, and sometimes her, own special recipe for the fertiliser needed to produce prize-winning monster gooseberries. For some it's sheep manure watered down, for others it's manure of any description. One competitor is even alleged to have buried a dead pig under his gooseberries so that the roots could take up nutrients from the blood and bone. What do these monster gooseberries taste like? Who knows? Who cares? They're not for eating …

ASPARAGUS

Once upon a time, the fertile Vale of Evesham was full of asparagus growers, and indeed of asparagus shows. Now much of the asparagus we buy comes from abroad, and there is only one asparagus fair left and that is in the Cotswold village of Bretforton.

To the accompaniment of the village band and in the atmosphere of a village fete, the asparagus is auctioned in the courtyard of the historic village inn, The Fleece, some in bundles, some in boxes. The star lot is always a box of a hundred and twenty heads called the 'Big One' and the layers are tied the traditional way with a piece of supple willow. In 1994, the Big One went for £110.

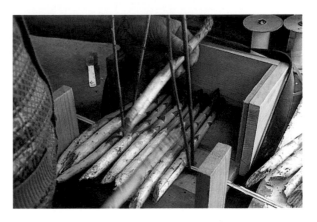

The asparagus sold in the auction is grown from seed. One-year-old plants are then set out 30cm (12in) apart, in rows just over 1m (3ft 3in) apart. As each one is planted, the bottom inch or so of the roots is torn off to make sure they don't turn up, but grow straight down to anchor the plant firmly. In the second year, a trench is dug between the rows and the soil from it is used to earth up the emerging spears on either side. The way to ensure a good crop according to grower Donald Halford is to 'keep it clean. If it gets full of weeds, it soon deteriorates.'

Presenter 1996 – 2002

Alan Titchmarsh

As with Roy Lancaster, it was a passion for nature and for wildlife that led the young Alan Titchmarsh to plants and gardening. Some of his earliest memories are of spending time on his grandfather's allotment in Ilkley – his enduring love for old fashioned plants, such as sweet peas and scabious, dates from then.

In his parents' back garden, he put up small polythene greenhouses in which he raised seeds bought with his pocket money, which was also spent on cacti from church bazaars, though a rubber plant at £3 was beyond his reach. His favourite television programme was *Gardening Club* and his boyhood hero was Percy Thrower – or 'Percy Chucker' as he and Mickey Hudson, his friend across the road, used to call him.

It was clear that all Alan wanted to do with his life was be a gardener, so he left school at fifteen with one 'O' level in

Art – having taken that a year early – and didn't bother taking the rest. He took a job in Ilkley Parks Department nursery as an apprentice gardener and studied for his City and Guilds in Horticulture at day release and in the evening. From there, he went horticultural college at Oaklands in Hertfordshire where he studied for the National Certificate in Horticulture.

This was followed by three years at the Royal Botanic Gardens, Kew, working for the prestigious Kew Diploma. He also got involved in local amateur dramatics, where productions such as *The Mikado* and *Half a Sixpence* honed his performance skills and also introduced him to his future wife Alison.

After he qualified, he stayed on at Kew for two years as supervisor of staff training and then went into journalism. His first job was editing gardening books with, among others, his boyhood hero Percy Thrower. He then became deputy editor of *Amateur Gardening*, and as money was tight, also moonlighted as 'Tom Derwent' and sometimes 'Richard Arncliffe' for his good friend Geoff Hamilton, then editor of the rival magazine *Practical Gardening*.

Alan was also keen to get into broadcasting, and when a letter arrived at *Amateur Gardening* asking if anyone would be interested in contributing to Radio 4's *You and Yours* as a gardening expert, Alan volunteered. His first item was on turf, and he was interviewed by Derek Cooper, who introduced him as 'Alan Titchfield'.

The greenfly plague that had hit Margate in the summer of 1979 proved a turning point. As a result of hearing him talk about it on the *Today* programme, *Nationwide* invited him to appear that evening to cover the same topic. They were most complimentary about his performance and said they would invite him back, which they did – twelve months later, after someone's roof garden had collapsed into the flat below. But this time it was only a week before he appeared again, in what was to become a regular slot and since then, he has rarely been off the screen, appearing in *Breakfast Time*, *Open Air*, *Pebble Mill*, *Songs of Praise*, *Titchmarsh's Travels*, *The Word* and the Chelsea Flower Show. The reason he worked on so many non-gardening programmes, Alan says, was simply because that's what he was offered, although he has found the experience of so much live television enormously useful. After coping with collapsing chairs and uncommunicative guests, an hour a night 'live' from the Chelsea Flower Show holds no terrors for him now.

1n 1996, in very difficult circumstances following the sudden death of his good friend Geoff Hamilton he took over as main presenter of *Gardeners' World* ,the job he had dreamed about when he was a boy.

The hugely popular *Ground Force*, for which Alan designed all the gardens as well presenting the programmes, began the following year, moving from BBC 2 onto BBC 1, and attracting audiences only slightly smaller than East Enders. More recently, the two series of *How To be A Gardener*, and *Going Back to Basics*, were also enormously popular.

As if making all these programmes wasn't enough, Alan had also embarked on a career as a novelist, and to date has written four, all best sellers and one of them winner of the Literary Review's Bad Sex Award. He has also written over thirty gardening books – one of them, *How to be A Gardener Part 1*, the fastest selling gardening book ever– and a volume of autobiography. In the spring of 2003, Alan had no less than three books in the non-fiction best sellers' list. He has also written for newspapers – the *Daily Mail* and currently the *Daily Express* and *Sunday Express* – and magazines such as *Radio Times* and *BBC Gardeners' World*. In January 2000, Alan was awarded the MBE for services to horticulture and broadcasting.

At the end of 2002, he decided it was time to move on, leaving both *Ground Force* and *Gardeners' World*. He had been offered two exciting projects – a series on Royal gardens and a landmark series on the natural history of the British Isles – and there were not enough days in the week to do everything. He also felt that he had gone as far as he could with *Ground Force* and since he was just about to move house and did not want the cameras in his new garden, he felt it was the right time to leave Gardeners' World. That does not mean that his gardening days are over. Making gardening programmes is what he enjoys most, and having dreamt as a boy of following Percy Thrower and becoming the Nation's Head Gardener, it's a title that he very much wants to keep.

The Winter
Garden

The Beauty of Winter

SNOW

Early in March in 1995, the crew arrived at Barnsdale to find it under a blanket of snow. Since Geoff Hamilton, like all good gardeners, believes that the best thing you can do for a garden in those conditions is keep off it, he was at first reluctant to go ahead with recording his links for the programme. Eventually, the director managed to persuade him to do his opening piece walking through the largely uncultivated woodland at the front of Barnsdale where little damage would be done.

The result was one of the most magical openings to the programme ever, as Geoff walked through trees whose bare branches were iced with fresh snow, and it looked like fairyland. It was important that he got it right first time because after that first walk through, the virgin snow would be virgin no more, with not only Geoff's footprints, but those of the cameraman, soundman and director too, all walking backwards in front of him. Geoff was glad to see the snow because he felt it had a cleansing effect of the garden, getting rid of a lot of the gardeners' enemies that survive mild winters.

COPING WITH SNOW

Keep off the garden, lawns in particular, because feet can break the frozen blades of grass, causing brown patches when the snow melts. Use a stick to knock snow off branches that are laden down with it because the weight can break them or bend them out of shape. If this happens to conifers, tie them back in with plastic-coated wire to the main stem, making sure you wrap sacking or a strip of old towelling round the branch and the trunk to prevent the wire digging in. Once the branch has settled back into position you can remove the wire.

Always trim hedges so that they are narrower at the top than the bottom to prevent snow settling on the top and the weight of it forcing the hedge open. If any depth does settle, it's worth knocking that off with a stick, too, just in case.

If you have a fruit cage in the garden and snow is forecast, roll the netting back, otherwise the weight of it covered in frozen snow can cause the whole structure to collapse.

FLOODS

In the last few years, flooding has become a hazard for gardeners far more frequently than before. In the spring of 1998, floods affected many parts of the country and, in some areas, one month's rain fell in just 24 hours, with the result that thousands of gardens were under water. Gardeners' World filmed the devastation in Robin and Sue Wensley's garden in Leamington Spa and Alan Titchmarsh offered advice to anyone else in the same situation.

COPING WITH FLOODS

First of all, safety. If the greenhouse is flooded, make sure the electricity is turned off and then leave it to dry out. If walls are knocked over, make them safe and then stack the bricks away from the plants until the weather is suitable for rebuilding.

Don't walk on the lawn or the borders. Leave them alone until the water level had dropped. If it's mainly dried out but there are still puddles, stab the area with a fork, then rake over the area to break up the mud. The grass will soon get going again.

If plants have been uprooted, pot them up in compost to drain off, and return them to the soil when they have recovered.

If vegetables and other seedlings have been washed away, don't panic. There's still time to sow again. Mud can prevent plants from 'breathing', so carefully remove it from the surface of the leaves, so that they can get the light and air they need to recover.

Joe Swift

Having left school and dropped out of art college with no idea of what he wanted to do with his life, Joe spent a year travelling round Europe and ended up working on a kibbutz in Israel. He'd enjoyed gardening as a child with his grandparents and his mother, the novelist Margaret Drabble, and when he got back to England, still no clearer about his future, he took a job with a firm of gardeners in north London. It was called Gaylord & Merryweather, founded and run by the actor who starred in the TV series *Zoo Vet*, and who is now a screenwriter, Rob Heyland.

After two years, he went to Australia to work as a landscaper in Sydney and Melbourne and was very taken with the completely different attitude there to outdoor space. When he came back to London, a friend asked him to design a garden. Realising he didn't have a clue how to set about it properly, he enrolled in the English Gardening School at the Chelsea Physic Garden to do a course in design.

Having then worked with a friend designing and building gardens, he set up The Plant Room in north London, which, until very recently, was a garden shop as well the base for his thriving garden design business. The design business is doing so well that he needed to expand into the space occupied by the shop. His first book, also called *The Plant Room*, was published in 2000.

City gardens are his speciality and he also writes a column called 'The Urban Jungle' for *The Independent*. He presented the second series of *Small Town Gardens* and still appears frequently on gardening programmes, including *Garden Invaders*, and coverage of the major flower shows.

Rachel de Thame

Certainly the most glamorous presenter in the programmes's thirty-five-year history, Rachel's career path to horticulture has been an unlikely one. Her first ambition was to be a ballet dancer, and she studied at the Royal Ballet School, but a prolonged bout of glandular fever forced her to abandon her dream. While she was marking time, working as a receptionist at a firm of international art dealers in London, she was spotted by a modelling agency, which led to a long and successful career as a model doing mainly photographic work. Appearances in television commercials lead on to acting roles in the mini-series *Merlin* and the British film *Bodywork*.

By now Rachel had two children and an acting career was not what she wanted. Since she had always loved gardening, and had spent much of her childhood visiting nurseries and gardens with her father who was a passionate plantsman, she enrolled at the English Gardening School at The Chelsea Physic garden.

There she earned a certificate in practical horticulture and plants and plantsmanship. As well as being a regular on Gardeners' World, Rachel presented the first series of the makeover series, *Small Town Gardens*, and in 2003, a series celebrating the work of The Royal Horticultural Society's gardeners, *Garden with the Experts*. She has also been a presenter on the coverage of the major flower shows Chelsea, Hampton Court, Gardeners' World Live and Tatton Park. She has written books to accompany both her series, as well as a book on her Top One Hundred Star Plants. She currently lives and gardens in London, but she's about to embark on creating a new country garden in Oxfordshire, which will be featured in a future TV series.

Organic
Gardening

Pippa Greenwood's Organic Vegetables

When *Gardeners' World* began, organic gardening was considered such a fringe activity that it barely featured in the programme. Percy Thrower was very keen on chemicals in the garden: The Magnolia's beds were always free of weeds, thanks to the then new weedkiller paraquat. Arthur Billitt was equally keen on chemicals to keep Clack's Farm perfect.

It was Geoff Hamilton who introduced organic gardening to *Gardeners' World*, (see page 58) and from the mid-eighties onwards, he was entirely organic.

In 2001 Pippa Greenwood started an organic vegetable plot for *Gardeners' World* at her home in Hampshire. It was 12 x 12m (40 x 40ft), divided into six beds – one large bed for the fruit, one triangular bed for odds and ends and four rectangular beds for different types of vegetable crops that would be rotated over a four-year cycle.

PIPPA'S GARDEN THROUGH ITS FIRST FEW MONTHS

The programme visited the garden many times during the course of the year.

February Organic growing depends on feeding the soil not the plant, so Pippa single-dug the whole plot – digging out a trench to a spade's depth, putting a layer of well-rotted manure in the bottom, and then filling it in with soil dug from a second trench immediately behind it.

March For carrots and parsnips, Pippa raked over a seed bed, removing any lumps and stones, then made a drill 1cm (½in) deep. Parsnips are poor germinators, so she sowed 2–4 seeds at each 'station' to give a better chance of at least one germinating. The stations were 7.5cm (3in) apart, in rows 20cm (8in) apart. Since they are also slow germinators, Pippa sowed some quick-maturing lettuces with them to make best use of the soil and to mark the location of the parsnips, making weeding much easier. She also planted onion 'sets' – small onion bulbs – heat-treated to help prevent bolting, 5–10cm (2–4 in) apart, in rows 25cm (10in) apart, with the necks just proud of the soil. If they are too proud, birds pull them out. In her heavy soil, garlic is sown on a ridge to ensure good drainage.

Early April Pippa pricked out tomato seedlings sown inside last month in individual pots, holding them by the seed leaves – the small oval ones that came through first – not the true leaves or the stem, which are easily damaged. Using multipurpose compost in 7.5 cm (3in) pots, she made a hole in the centre, dropped each seedling in, firmed compost around the roots and stem with a dibber and watered them well.

Late April The club-root resistant calabrese variety 'Trixie', sown in individual cells or modules a few weeks earlier, were thinned to the strongest seedling in each. Pippa planted them outside, 15cm (6in) apart, in rows 30cm (12 in) apart, and covered them with horticultural fleece. It allows light and water through but keeps pests, like cabbage root fly, aphids, caterpillars and pigeons, out.

Early May Pippa sowed her peas in a flat-bottomed trench about 5cm (2in) deep, about 10cm (4in) apart and in three rows the same distance apart. She filled in with soil and firmed it well. Since birds love the tender young shoots, she protected the rows with expanding polythene cloches, which keep off excess rain too.
She started off her courgettes inside by sowing the individual seeds on their sides about 2–2.5cm (½–1in) deep in pots of compost. She also started her runner beans in trays, placing the seeds about 5cm (2in) apart and pushing them down into the compost.

Pippa also made wigwams from bamboo canes to support the runner beans when they go outside when all danger of frost is past. She stressed the importance of pushing the canes well into the soil – at least 30cm (12in), since a crop of runner beans can be very weighty.

Late May Pippa planted out sweetcorn that she sowed indoors a few weeks earlier, four seeds to a 10cm (4in) pot. The plants need a sunny spot outside, and are best planted about 38cm (15 in) apart. Since sweetcorn is wind-pollinated, it's best grown in a block rather than in rows. With all danger of frost past, it was also time to plant out outdoor tomatoes and courgettes.

The young peas were through and about 7.5cm (3in) high, so it was time to remove the cloche and put in some twiggy pea sticks close enough to form a 'hedge' along both sides of the row.

Pippa's organic tips for keeping slugs and snails at bay

Mulch around the plants with cocoa shells, which have sharp edges and which the slugs and snails dislike crawling over.

Water the soil with nematodes (microscopic eelworms), which bury into slugs' bodies under the soil and destroy them.

Sink beer traps into the soil. Yogurt pots filled with beer will do. Always leave the traps about an inch proud of the soil to prevent ground beetles, which are allies in the fight against slugs and other pests, from falling in.

Bob Flowerdew's Organic Fruit

Bob's tips for pest control

Make a small pond in a kitchen garden to attract creatures like frogs and toads that eat pests such as slugs.

Putting up nesting boxes for birds also encourages them into the fruit garden where they will eat pests.

Make hibernation sites for beneficial insects like ladybirds or lacewings. A bundle of dead raspberry canes wrapped in newspaper and pushed into a plastic bottle with the shoulders cut off would serve very well.

Companion planting also helps. Herbs such as rosemary, thyme sage and chives attract beneficial insects to the area to eat pests. In the case of chives, they also draw sulphur from the soil, and make it available to the crops, bringing some immunity to fungus diseases.

Marigolds, and especially French marigolds (*Tagetes*), have a scent that drives away many unwanted insects. Their roots also exude a substance that kills some soil pests.

In 1995, Bob set up a fruit garden at his Norfolk home especially for *Gardeners' World*. There were some existing fruit trees but, as the focus of the new garden was to be soft fruit, a fruit cage was essential for crops such as raspberries, blackcurrants and strawberries, which were most at risk from the birds. Less vulnerable crops, like redcurrants and white currants, were grown outside.

RASPBERRIES

Bob suggests that you should plant bare-rooted canes in the autumn, and always look for those with a vigorous root system and the beginnings of new shoots that will produce next season's canes. Don't plant them too deeply, he says, and make sure you spread the roots out well. Cut them hard back to about 30cm (12in) after planting to encourage really strong, productive canes next year. Bob uses a simple post-and-wires system of support. Using two thin strands of wire together means that you can support each cane by putting it between the two wires and twisting them together either side of it.

STRAWBERRIES

Autumn is the time to plant them bare-rooted, and they should not be planted too deeply. The crown of the plant should not be buried. Although it's hard to do, you should pick off all the flowers in their first season to allow the energy to go into making strong plants rather than fruit. Being human though, Bob left a few flowers on one plant of each variety just to see what the fruit tasted like.

Bob's trademark, old tyres, had a part to play here – in his strawberry wall. The tyres were piled up like bricks, with a piece of old carpet placed in the bottom of each one so that the compost would not fall through the resulting gaps. Each tyre needs to be firmly stuffed with compost, and then you need one plant in each of the curved sections down the front of the wall, and two in each tyre at the top. Keep them well watered and, since the fruit is off the ground away from slugs and the damp air that can cause fungus diseases, you'll be rewarded with an earlier, cleaner, sweeter crop.

REDCURRANTS

These are very easy to grow and produce a massive crop with little attention. It's worth thinning them out in July.

Leave the main leaders and reduce all the other shoots by three-quarters. This means the plant's energy goes into next year's fruit production rather than vegetative growth.

GRAPES

The old textbooks say that individual bunches of grapes on indoor vines ought to the thinned out in August or September, but Bob believes life is too short for that and so he thins out whole bunches instead. As a rule of thumb, he suggests leaving one square foot of foliage for every bunch you want to ripen. As for outdoor grapes, he sees little point in thinning those since you may well only get relatively small grapes anyway.

TREE FRUIT

The 'June drop', which usually happens in July in Bob's part of the world, is the time when apples and pears drop most of the diseased, damaged or under-sized fruitlets – a process Bob assists by giving the trees a vigorous shake. He also goes one stage further by thinning out some of the healthy fruitlets, to allow fewer but larger fruits to reach maturity and ripen. It may seem wasteful but, in fact, you end up with the same weight of fruit only in fewer units. If you have a problem with aphids on fruit trees, check the trunk very carefully and you will almost certainly find columns of ants running up and down. They are 'farming' the aphids, moving them around the plant to feed and then taking the honeydew they produce. Stop the ants by fixing a band of tinfoil tightly around the trunk, fastening it with sticky tape and then coating it generously with tree-banding grease. This will make sure that the ants come to a sticky end, and the aphids will eventually disappear.

Chris Beardshaw

Presenter 2000 – Present

By the age of four, Chris Beardshaw was already fascinated by plants and especially seeds, growing everything from cress to sycamore. He hated being indoors and at every possible opportunity, he would be outside roaming the countryside. In his teens, he spent his weekends working in garden centres, learning about plants and giving advice to customers. Never in any doubt about what he wanted to do with his life, he studied landscape architecture and then went on to train in horticulture at Pershore College in Worcestershire. He stayed on as a lecturer, teaching students to degree level, specialising in landscape design, planting design and landscape history.

Chris has his own garde- design practice, through which he has designed both public and private spaces, ranging in size from regional reclamation schemes to pocket-handkerchief gardens. He has also designed exhibition gardens at national shows. Perhaps the highlight came in 1999 when he was awarded a gold medal for the Dig For Victory garden at the Chelsea Flower Show, on which he collaborated with Sir Terence Conran. More recently, he also led a team of amateurs to a gold medal and Best in Show award at *Gardeners' World* Live.

As well as *Gardeners' World*, Chris has also presented a garden history series, *Hidden Gardens*, *Gardening Neighbours* and several series of *The Flying Gardener*, in which the skills he has honed as hobbies – climbing, diving, canoeing – play almost as a big a part as his horticultural knowledge. His first book, *The Natural Gardener*, published in the spring of 2003 is based on the series.

He has just moved into a new home, a Victorian folly near Cheltenham, with a third of an acre of derelict garden, which he plans to renovate very slowly as a long-term project, not a quick fix makeover.

Monty Don

Monty Don is the first main *Gardeners' World* presenter to be completely self-taught. Born in 1955 to an army family, he was brought up in the Hampshire countryside, which he loved, and was never happier than when he was outdoors. At seventeen, he left home to live in the south of France where he worked as a jobbing gardener and played rugby for local clubs.

When he returned to England after a year, he worked on a succession of farms, before deciding to try, at twenty-one, to get into Cambridge. There he read English, played cricket and rugby, and earned a half-blue at boxing. Having met his future wife, Sarah, at Cambridge, he did a variety of jobs, including waiting tables while she studied jewellery design. In 1982 they started Monty Don Jewellery, which was a huge success. During the mid-1980s, no self-respecting earlobe was without its crystal-drop-and-velvet bow, trademark Monty Don earring.

During this time, Monty and Sarah – he insists theirs is an equal partnership – made their first garden together in London, which attracted such attention that he was asked to write about gardening for the *Mail on Sunday* and to present gardening items on *This Morning* with Richard and Judy. They had also embarked on a country garden, a forty-acre estate in Herefordshire. But then the '87 stock market crash saw the business run into serious trouble, and they lost everything, including the much-loved house

in Herefordshire – a story that's told movingly in Monty's first book *The Prickotty Bush*. TV work and journalism dried up, and Monty, having suffered with clinical depression for much of his life, found himself unable to function. He sought help and a combination of anti-depressants and cognitive therapy helped him recover. In 1993, a legacy enabled them to buy another house in Herefordshire – condemned as unfit for human habitation. They set about restoring it and, just as importantly, creating another garden, a more modest two acres this time.

On the day they moved in, Monty was offered more television work, and since then, he hasn't stopped. As well as *This Morning*, there has been *The Holiday Programme*; and several gardening series for Channel 4 including *Real Gardens*, *Fork to Fork* (a gardening and cookery series with Sarah), and for three years, The Chelsea Flower Show. He has written a weekly gardening column for the *Observer* for eight years, and has published a number of books, most recently *The Complete Gardener*.

He is a great believer in the therapeutic value of gardening for people suffering from mental illness – in particular, the gentle physical exercise and the satisfaction found in completing small tasks. He shares with Geoff Hamilton the belief that helping people to garden offers a way of enriching every aspect of their lives.

Doyennes of
Gardening

Miss Ellen Willmott

In 1992, Liz Rigbey visited Warley Place in Essex on the trail of the remarkable woman gardener, Ellen Willmott, who, at the end of the nineteenth and beginning of the twentieth centuries, turned Warley Place into one of the most famous gardens in Europe.

ABOVE: Fewer than half of the 104 gardeners Miss Willmott employed.

Her wealthy father, Frederick, a lawyer and businessman, had bought the house in 1875 when Ellen was seventeen and not longer after, she had taken control of the grounds. The layout of the gardens was informal: she was a great follower of William Robinson and of Gertrude Jekyll (who generously called her 'the greatest of living women gardeners'), the two great champions of the wild garden. Within it there was every kind of garden that the Victorians admired – Japanese and Chinese gardens, rose beds, a fernery, an orchid house and other hot houses. There was also an alpine garden, for which Miss Willmott brought over a young Swiss gardener, Jacob Moreau, a venture that was to end in tragedy.

Miss Willmott's ambitions for the garden were only possible because she had a great fortune at her disposal. She employed a staggering one hundred and four gardeners, dressed in the uniform she had designed for them, which included green, knitted-silk ties and navy blue aprons, and was a hard task master. They all worked twelve hour days in the week and ten hours on Saturdays and she was often to be found stalking the gardens checking up on their work.

Miss Willmott also got her own hands dirty too. She was a practical gardener with a fondness for breeding plants. She grew, for example, acres of daffodils, protected from plant poachers by trip wires rigged to air guns. She funded plant-hunting expeditions abroad and propagated many of the plants brought back. She took great delight in the fact that she often managed to grow plants that even Kew Gardens could not.

She also became a great authority on roses, and set out to produce the definitive guide, *The Genus Rosa*. She attempted to classify every rose, but found herself often baffled by the intricacies of rose parenthood. When the beautifully produced volumes of *The Genus Rosa* were finally published in 1914, at her own expense, they were already out of date. They sold poorly and lost money.

As well as pouring money into Warley Place, Miss Willmott had also bought homes abroad in Italy and France, and spent vast amounts of money on them too. By the time the First World War began, she was in serious financial difficulty.

> She could no longer afford to pay her gardeners, most of whom had been called up, and had to stand by helplessly while nature took its course. As she herself had once written, 'Who among us can fool ourselves that we do more than borrow our gardens from nature.'

She died in 1934 and a few years later the house was pulled down. Miss Willmott's ghost lives on though, as the common name to the silvery, thistle-like *Eryngium*

giganteum, so called because she used to scatter seed of it surreptitiously in gardens she visited. There were plans to develop the grounds but they came to nothing and, in the end, the gardens went to rack and ruin. The creator of her alpine garden, Jacob Moreau, committed suicide, partly in despair at the destruction of his life's work.

Eventually, the Essex Wildlife Trust took it over and they still manage it today as a wildlife sanctuary.
There is virtually no trace left of the garden.

BELOW: Liz Rigbey among Miss Willmott's daffodils.

Penelope Hobhouse

Penelope Hobhouse, who was born in Northern Ireland in 1929, is an internationally renowned garden writer, garden designer, garden historian, lecturer and gardener.

Her name is perhaps still most closely associated with Tintinhull House in Somerset, the National Trust garden she transformed over her fourteen-year tenure, along with her husband, the late Professor John Malins. *Gardeners' World* visited her there in 1993, just before she left Tintinhull to embark on creating a brand new garden of her own.

She first saw Tintinhull, as laid out and planted by the late Mrs Sybil Reiss, when she was in her late twenties and it was a revelation that changed her life. 'It was the first time I realised that gardening was about beauty, not just about deadheading and keeping things tidy, and when I came to live here in 1979, I wanted passionately to make the garden as beautiful as it had been then, in Mrs Reiss's day.' At the beginning, she and her husband found it rather difficult to stick to the plant lists that the National Trust provided. 'We felt strongly that had Mrs Reiss still been alive she would have liked to experiment, so gradually we did start experimenting and hoped that the Trust wouldn't notice.'

Tintinhull was the perfect place for Penelope Hobhouse to garden because she loves the combination of strict geometry – straight paths and right angles – with plants billowing over the edges to create a feeling of softness. 'Most people are immensely keen on not having too much work to do in their gardens, and I hope that they've got through the idea that wild gardens or meadow gardens are going to involve no work because they are the most labour intensive of all.

In fact, I think people will come round to a style of garden a little bit like Tintinhull, with definite straight paths and angles and hedges for structure because you can garden

it much more simply than we do. We're gardeners and we do it because we love it.'

Even so, with a minimal staff to look after it, Penelope had learned to simplify some parts of the garden. The iris beds, for example, used to involve someone weeding on their hands and knees at least six times in the summer. 'For that reason this used to be my least favourite part of the garden but then we started cheating a little, and put in alliums under the iris rhizomes. Then suddenly I had the idea of scattering nigella seed through it all. I must admit the irises have not done as well, but I just love it.' Colour is important to her, too, and indeed her first major book was called *Colour In Your Garden*. 'It was a wonderful book to write here because I could experiment. I did things like rushing outside at night in my nightdress to see if white flowers really do glow in the dark. They do.'

When you are designing a border for yourself, she believes, most people begin with one plant. 'Perhaps you've seen a blue ceanothus that you just must have, so you have to think about what would go with that. Perhaps the acid-lime greenish yellow of *Euphorbia characias*, because blue and yellow are complementary colours. Then it's like making a painting, building up a composition, not just with flowers, but the shape and colour of leaves and texture too matters a great deal.'

While gardening is her life, she still finds it extremely difficult. 'One thinks about it night and day and it doesn't get any easier. Sometimes you have great successes and sometimes great failures but the good thing about it is that there's always next year. That's what makes gardening possible.'

Beth Chatto

When Beth Chatto embarked on making a garden near Colchester in Essex in 1960, on a steep, dry, sunbaked bank sloping down to a muddy ditch, she quickly discovered that the only way to tackle difficult sites was to choose plants that thrived naturally in those conditions – to work with nature rather than to try to fight it.

The fact that this seems like basic common sense now is a tribute to the influence Beth Chatto has had in the last forty years on the way we garden. She has also been influential in drawing our attention to the fact that the form and shape of a plant, and the texture and colour of its leaves, are just as important as the colour of its flowers and, of course, they have a far longer season of interest. Graceful, arching plants, big-leaved plants and grasses create eye-catching contrasts, while tall plants lift the eye and create an ideal background for other plants.

Gardeners' World has paid many visits to Beth's garden over the years, starting in May 1980 with Clay Jones and Geoffrey Smith, to look at the water garden, the bog garden, the different woodland gardens, and the Mediterranean garden. The programme made several visits to the new gravel garden from 1993 onwards, firstly with Nick Wray, and most recently with Stephan Lacey in 1998.

This remarkable experiment in ecological gardening was inspired by seeing dried-up river beds in California and by Derek Jarman's extraordinary shingle garden on the beach at Dungeness in Kent.

The gravel garden began in the winter of 1991–92, when Beth had three-quarters of an acre of what had been the car park dug up and the thin, stony soil improved with a hundred tons of organic matter and bonfire waste. It was planned as a series of sweeping curves to reinforce the idea of a meandering, dried-up river bed and because, Beth said, it was not a setting for a formal garden and there wasn't a straight line anywhere. Then it was planted with a range of drought-tolerant evergreens, such as

cistus, bergenias and euphorbias, and evergreys, like lavender, artemisia and *Ballota*, as well as drought-resistant grasses, such as *Stipa gigantea*, *Festuca glauca* and *Helictotrichon*. Structure in the planting was important. 'I looked around to see where it needed height and then planted something vertical like a juniper, *Juniperus scopulorum* 'Skyrocket', or Mount Etna broom, *Genista aetnensis*, to lead the eye.

The planting doesn't then rise in increasing steps towards them – that can look heavy and rather wodgy. I used a lot of lower planting, like silvery *Ballota* and santolina, sometimes right through to the back.' Bulbs, such as alliums and species tulips, add seasonal colour and, in winter, evergreen *Phlomis*, along with other evergreens, gives structure.

The garden has never been watered, even in times of drought, which are frequent in Essex with only 50cm (20in) of rain a year and yet, far from looking arid, the flowing drifts of planting are full of colour and interest.

Rosemary Verey

During her lifetime tens of thousands of visitors came to see the garden every year, to admire not just the laburnum walk, but also the intricate knot gardens and the potager, the decorative formal fruit and vegetable plot that started the fashion for small, attractive kitchen gardens. Since Barnsley House was sold in 2002, it is only open to the public on half a dozen days a year.

Rosemary Verey, another of the most influential garden designers and gardeners in the latter part of the 20th century, was completely self-taught, but was born with a marvellous eye for colour, line, and texture. Over the years, she added to that a knowledge of and feeling for plants that only experience can bring, as well as detailed study of garden history.

Her garden at Barnsley House in Gloucestershire, which she developed over 30 years, was her schoolroom and her laboratory, and became – justifiably – famous all round the world. When her husband David inherited the house in 1951, she knew little about gardening and, with a young family to raise, had little time. It was only when the children went away to school that her interest in gardening began.

In 1961, David invited the famous designer Percy Cane to look at the garden and offer advice. Rosemary had been reluctant to make a start on the garden, but his visit was the spur she needed. She wanted to design the garden herself. One vital piece of advice she did absorb from Percy Cane was the importance of creating as many vistas, as long as possible, regardless of the garden's size. That advice is made manifest at Barnsley House with its many vistas, perhaps most famously the view to the temple beyond the formal pool, and, of course, the laburnum arch underplanted with purple alliums with a simple stone sundial at the end, which is one of the most photographed of all garden features. She and David were given the laburnums as a silver wedding present in 1964 and he laid the cobble path beneath it as a present to her.

Another huge formative influence on her was the book *The Education of a Gardener* by Russell Page which, she said, taught her how to see – how to look inside flowers, to look at the shapes that plants make, the horizontals and the verticals, to consider how to mould everything together, to make a garden that has in it nothing jarring. 'That and the fact that everyone has to be a beginner at some time and so not to be daunted.'

It was the desire to share with other people the joy that gardening gave her that started her writing, first articles then books such as *The Garden in Winter*, *Good Planting* and *Rosemary Verey's Garden Plans*. 'It was not because I thought I know best, but from wanting in a very humble way for people to get the same joy from what they themselves can do.'

The writing and then lecturing, here and in the USA, led, inevitably, to people inviting her to their gardens and asking advice on what to plant where. She started drawing sketches on the backs of envelopes and the designing started from there. But it was doing planting plans, and the planting that she loved best. Despite including clients such as the Prince of Wales, Elton John and Anne Robinson among her clients, she always found big layouts extremely difficult.

She died on May 31st, 2001 of pneumonia. She was 82.

Bugs, Slugs &
Other Thugs

Pests and Diseases

Many garden pests are as old as gardening itself – slugs and snails, aphids, earwigs and so on – but during the years *Gardeners' World* has been on the air, and as the climate has slowly changed, new pests have come to prominence.

VINE WEEVILS

In 1999, Pippa Greenwood tackled vine weevils, a pest that has been steadily increasing in numbers over the last few years and devastating gardens all over the country. The dark, grey-brown adults make characteristic notches on the edges of leaves, which is unsightly but does the plant no real harm. The creamy white grubs, on the other hand, which eat away at the root system, are far more devastating. Plants die suddenly, for no obvious reason, and then you find that the entire root system has been eaten away. Plants in containers are particularly susceptible because the weevil grubs are in a confined space, feeding on just one root system, and also they are less likely run into one of their main natural predators, the ground beetle.

Vine weevils are very hard to get rid of. There are no males, and each female can lay between 800–1600 eggs. This means that even if you fail to kill just one weevil you will still have a major infestation the following year. Roll up pieces of corrugated cardboard and secure with an elastic band. Lay them around your containers. Vine weevils need somewhere dark to hide during the day. Unwrap the cardboard and dispose of the vine weevils in any way you like.

Stand pots on a pot feet in a shallow tray of water – vine weevils can't swim and so can't reach them. Look out for and encourage ground beetles as they eat weevil grubs. Always inspect plants carefully before buying them. If possible take the plant out of its pot and check for grubs curled up on the root ball. Use special compost impregnated with an insecticide called imidacloprid.

NEW ZEALAND FLATWORMS

Every gardener knows how important earthworms are to the health of the soil, dragging organic matter down into it and, with their casts, helping to turn it over. So any serious threat to the earthworm population affects farmers and gardeners alike. In 1994, Pippa Greenwood revealed just such a threat – the New Zealand flatworm (*Arthurdendyus triangulatus*). It's dark brown to black in colour, covered in slime and can reach up to 20cm (8in) in length – and it eats earthworms. The manner in which it does so is particularly disgusting. It sidles up alongside an earthworm, lies on top of it, enveloping it, and then produces a poison that paralyses it. Next, it covers the earthworm in digestive juices and then sucks up the resulting soup.

Flatworms like to curl up in cool moist places under stones, for example, and also in potted plants between the compost and the pot. Its egg capsule, which looks like a small black olive, harbours up to seven embryos, so each one is almost an infestation in its own right.

They were first noticed in this country in Northern Ireland in 1963, thought to have been brought in among a shipment of plants from New Zealand. By 1965, they had spread to Scotland to be found mainly in botanical gardens, nurseries and gardens. They rapidly spread throughout Northern Ireland and Scotland but, by 1994, had only penetrated England as far as Manchester, Harrogate, Carlisle and Harrow.

Almost ten years later, isolated sightings have been reported throughout England and Wales, caused mainly, it is believed, by people bringing plants from a 'hot spot' to an area that was previously clear. But as the worms seem to prefer it cool and damp, the problem remains mostly concentrated in Northern Ireland and Scotland.

There is no chemical control against them that does not also kill earthworms, and there are no natural predators. They can be trapped by leaving a paving slab or a sack of compost on the soil and inspecting the underside every morning for coiled flatworms. They can be disposed of in salted water or they can be squashed. Cutting them up only increases the population. Please do report any sightings to Department of the Environment, Food and Rural Affairs (DEFRA) on their website: www.defra.gov.uk

LILY BEETLE

The lily beetle with its bright lacquer-red body, black head and black legs is one of the most striking-looking of all insect pests, but its charm rapidly wears off when it

devastates your lilies. As Pippa Greenwood reported in 1992, the lily beetle, which is common in Europe, is thought to have arrived in Surrey from where it has spread throughout the south east of England and is slowly moving north.

The adults will feed extensively on the leaves, stems and even flowers of lilies and related species, like fritillaries, lily-of-the valley (*Convallaria*) and Solomon's Seal (*Polygonatum*), and so do the grubs, revolting-looking black creatures, which look like bird droppings and indeed are covered in their own excrement.

The female can lay between two and three hundred eggs in a season. These are tiny and scarlet in colour, turning brown as they age, and are usually laid on the lower surface of the leaves. It is possible to spray them with a contact insecticide, but since they go on appearing throughout the summer, you need to spray every seven to fourteen days to keep the problem under control.

The organic solution is to inspect the plants regularly, picking off the adults, grubs and eggs as soon as you see them. Watch out, though – when you disturb the foliage, the adults often drop to the ground and scuttle away and, despite their brilliant colour, they are not easy to spot.

Index